INTRODUCING WEST NEW GUINEA

New Guinea Communications

Volume 4

KAL MULLER

INTRODUCING WEST NEW GUINEA

NEW GUINEA COMMUNICATIONS

Volume 4

GALDA VERLAG 2021

ISBN 978-3-96203-175-6 (Print)
ISBN 978-3-96203-176-3 (Ebook)

Bibliografische Information der Deutschen Nationalbibliothek
Die Deutsche Nationalbibliothek verzeichnet diese Publikation in der Deutschen Nationalbibliografie; detaillierte bibliografische Daten sind im Internet über http://dnb.ddb.de abrufbar.

© 2021 Galda Verlag, Glienicke
Neither this book nor any part may be reproduced or transmitted in any form or by any means electronic or mechanical, including photocopying, micro-filming, and recording, or by any information storage or retrieval system, without prior permission in writing from the publisher. Direct all inquiries to Galda Verlag, Franz-Schubert-Str. 61, 16548 Glienicke, Germany

NEW GUINEA COMMUNICATIONS
A SERIES

The aim is to provide a conduit for the publication of studies on the Island of New Guinea, with its two established political divisions, but will also include other associated patterns of islands.

It will enable contributions from new knowledge workers—with their dissertations—and from established scholars. As there are numerous scholars who would like better coverage of the areas in which they have explored—as a tribute to the people they have worked with—as well as local scholars who understand the importance of their unique areas. It is felt that the approaches being trialed in the visual anthropology part of the series as area studies will bring a wider attention to the remarkable nature of the island.

The first volumes will be on modes of communication: oral history and folklore, and the emergence of a local literature. While the representation of all disciplines is welcome, comparative and whole island studies would be of great interest as well. For this, collaborative works or edited volumes may be needed.

It will allow for academic publications of a more preliminary kind—rather than exhaustive monographs, which are becoming more and more impossible to produce.

Where is the knowledge we have lost?

John Evans
SERIES DEVELOPER
BOOK2BUK2PLES LTD.

FOREWORD

This book was written for anyone interested in the history and cultures of West New Guinea. Future books will cover the area's three major divisions: the highlands, the north coast and the south coast.

I wrote this Introduction to West New Guinea while employed by Freeport Indonesia as a consultant. I very much want to thank this mining company for having given me the time and opportunity to produce this book and other books. My position with Freeport allowed me to travel to many parts of West New Guinea easily for photography and research.

The idea of this book received the enthusiastic support from Dr. Agus Sumule of the UNIPA University of Manokwari. Together, we had already published a book on the biodiversity of West New Guinea. Both the West New Guinea government and Freeport supported us in that project.

Three experts in the field of Papuan studies read my manuscript: Dr. Alex Szaly, Dr. Chris Ballard and Dr. Anton Ploeg. Their suggestions have been incorporated in the text and the mistakes they pointed out were rectified. Dr. Ballard and Dr. Ploeg took time from their extremely busy schedules to provide essential information through many emails. I have used comments and information throughout the text, sometimes without attribution, for which I apologize.

I will attempt to describe the physical environment in which the various Papuan groups live, cover their lifestyles and concentrate on their traditional cultures, many elements of which are in the process of disappearing if not already gone since shortly after contact with the outside world. Most of the contents of this book are a distillation of what has been written and published by linguists, anthropologists and archeologists in the English language. As this book was written for a general public and not an academic one, I kept attributions to a minimum in the text. The most important books I consulted are in the bibliography.

My own experience of several years was centered on the Kamoro group of the south coast and the Amungme in the highlands. I also studied the Dani, the Lani, the Moni, the Wodani, the Me and the Ok during brief periods but had no direct contact with the Mek and the Yali.

INTRODUCTION

Papuans can well be proud of the accomplishments of their ancestors. There is no reason for any feelings of inferiority just because, until relatively recently, many Papuans still *'lived in the Stone Age'*. The lack of technological advances did not preclude a rich and complex set of cultures with highly developed agriculture allowing for large populations with important and complex rituals. Modern agricultural technology has not been able to improve yields from the highly efficient traditional farming methods in many areas, including the Baliem Valley, Kolopom/Dolak Island and elsewhere.

Papuans were among the first peoples on earth to begin agriculture. They domesticated sugar cane, a strain of bananas, and cultivated root crops (yams and taro) long before there was any farming in Java. Surplus food allowed the large-scale rearing of pigs, essential for huge feasts in the highlands. Many groups participated in tribal warfare, but a lack of advanced weapons technology kept down the number of deaths. Some groups had practices that were repugnant to Europeans, such as cannibalism, ritual homosexuality and group heterosexuality. But we must not look at these practices as perverted in any sense of the term as they fit in with their spiritual beliefs in sustaining life and fertility.

Throughout this book, we use the term 'Papuan' to refer to today's indigenous inhabitants (as well as plants and animals) of the island of New Guinea. These Papuans are the now mixed descendants of two waves of migrations: a very early one from Africa and a much later one from Taiwan. The word 'Melanesian', literally meaning 'black inhabitants of islands', encompasses a wider geographical area than just New Guinea. Thus, while all Papuans could be called Melanesians, not all Melanesians are Papuans.

CONTENTS

New Guinea Communications　v
Foreword　vii
Introduction　ix

1 Geology, geography and climate 2
　The breakup of Pangea 4
　New Guinea emerges... 5
　The highlands of the central mountain range 6
　The Bird's Head 8

2 Biodiversity 10
　Mammals 14
　Crocodiles and their kin 15
　Essential fish life.. 16
　Birds-of-paradise 16
　Many insects, some useful, others not 18
　Mollusks 19
　Plant life 19

3 Migration from Africa to New Guinea 22
　Papuan pioneers in New Guinea............................. 26

4 Migration from Asia: the Austronesians become Melanesians (Lapita culture)..............28
　The Austronesians in New Guinea 31
　A vexing question: the timing of the pigs' first arrival.. 33
　What does Melanesia really mean?......................... 34
　A winning combination: the Melanesians 35
　The language factor... 37

5 Coastal and highland contrasts 40
　Pigs and sweet potatoes.. 42
　Trading: salt, cowries and stone blades 43

6   Early coastal trade with the outside world 46

    Lapita and Dongson long-range trading 48
    Trade with Indonesia 49
    Biak: Metal trade and forging 50
    Traders from Seram 51

7   European annexation, new values and their inland expansion 54

    The first explorers 57
    Attempts at colonization 59
    How The Netherlands acquired West New Guinea 60
    How West New Guinea became part of the Dutch East Indies 62
    Bases for colonial claims 62
    The Europeans venture inland 63
    Large-scale expeditions to the central mountains from the south 65
    The British team 66
    Expeditions to the central mountains from the north 68
    The first use of an airplane in exploring West New Guinea 69
    The Colijn Expedition of 1936 70
    The Archbold expedition discovers the Baliem Valley 71
    The Papuan view 73

8   Opening of the highlands 76

    The Bijlmer expedition 79
    Enarotali: the first government post in the highlands 80
    Einar Mickelson: evangelical missionary 81
    Religious competition: Roman Catholics and Protestants 83
    Two versions of Christianity in West New Guinea 84

9   World War II in West New Guinea 88

    MacArthur and the War 91
    Beyond Hollandia 93

BIBLIOGRAPHY 96

PHOTOGRAPHS

Alpine lake formed by melted glaciers 2

Puncak Jaya 4884 m. 3

Butterflies abound in the lowlands 10

Pig-nosed turtle 11

Coconut crab, Raja Ampat Islands 13

Portrait of an Amungme man 22

Portrait of an Asmat 23

Beach on Biak Island 28

A young Biak girl 29

Singeing pig bristles 40

A tree house of the Korowai 41

Kamoro canoes with sails 46

Massoi bark at Lake Yamur 47

An Amungme dance group 54

Underground mining at Freeport 55

Lake Paniai and Enarotali town 76

Shrimp endemic to Lake Paniai 77

US troops landed here in WW II 88

DeBruijn and team 89

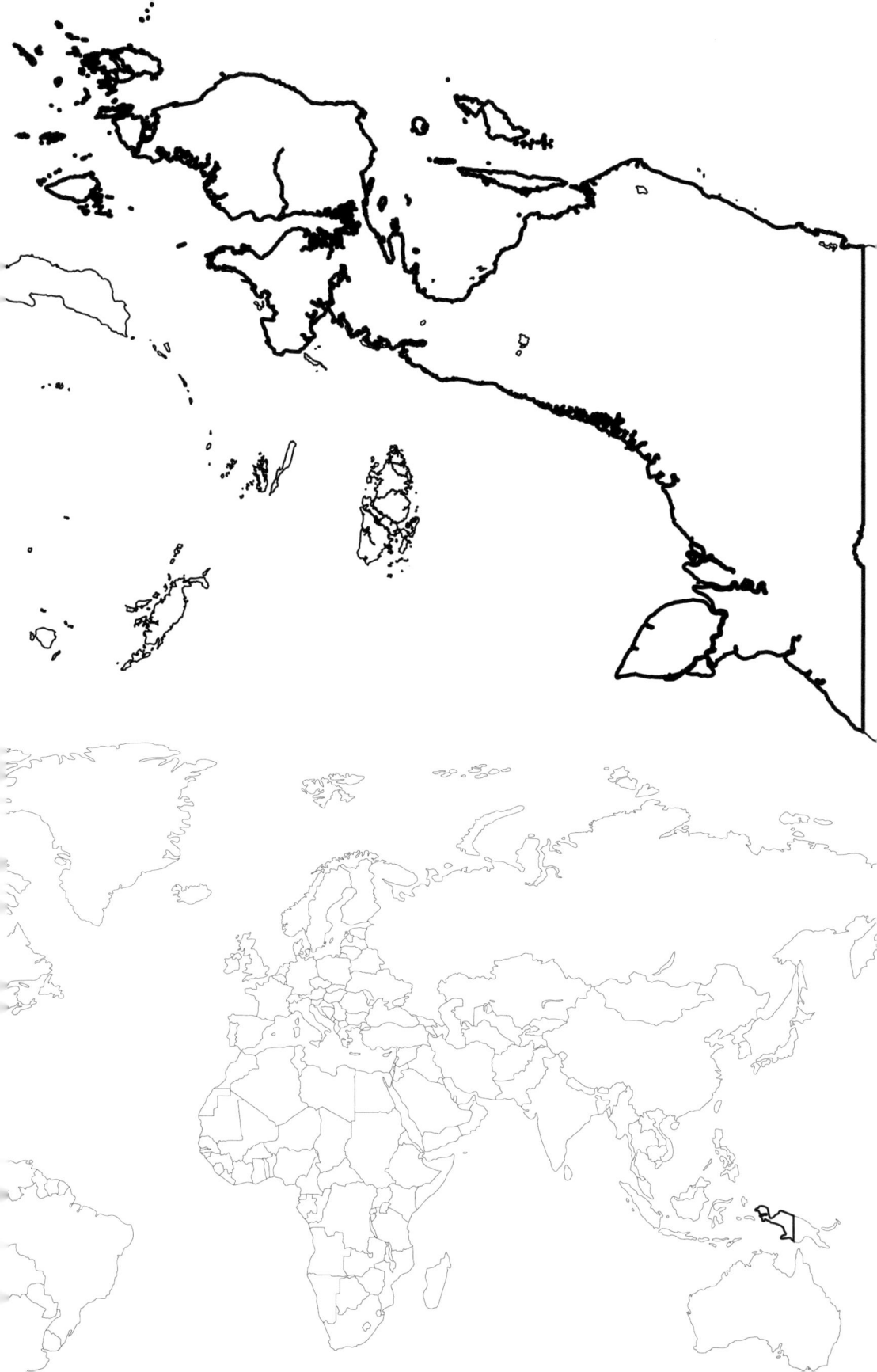

What to call this huge chunk of land? The western half of New Guinea Island has undergone a number of name changes. In colonial times, it was Netherlands [Dutch] New Guinea, then under Indonesian control it became Irian Barat, then Irian Jaya, then Papua. The province split into West Papua (the Bird's Head area), and just Papua for the rest up to the international border with the now independent country of Papua New Guinea (PNG). That country was made up of the former British colony called Papua and the former German Colony, New Guinea. Within the area considered in this book, the name West Papua is generally applied. But to outsiders this name might create confusion. So we decided to go with the geographical designation of West New Guinea.

Alpine glacier lake in West New Guinea located a few hundred meters above Freeport's Grasberg mine. Lakes hold waters from melting glaciers; migrating ducks land on the lakes.

GEOLOGY, GEOGRAPHY AND CLIMATE

1

Puncak Jaya, formerly Carstensz Peak, reaches 4884 m. It is the highest mountain between the Andes and the Himalayas.

The surface of our planet has changed drastically since the Earth was formed some 4.5 billion years ago. The earliest time, before the first appearance of life, is sometimes called '*Hadean*' a word based on the ancient Greek mythological designation for the underground home of the dead. Later, the term came to mean '*hell*'. For close to a billion years, the surface of the Earth was far too hot to support any form of life. Very slowly, a thin crust formed over the molten mass inside the earth. This crust, or landmass, floated around on the molten material beneath it. It is still floating today. Thus, land masses and oceans were never permanently fixed in their present positions. In fact, continents are still drifting and changing their relative positions, albeit at speeds of only a few centimeters per century, about the speed of a growing fingernail. But those centimeters can add up when we consider time spans of dozens or hundreds of millions of years.

We will skip over the early history of the Earth to look at its surface some 200 million years ago. The geological term for this period is called the Jurassic, otherwise known as the Age of the Dinosaurs. At that time, all of today's continents formed a single landmass, called Pangea. Shortly afterwards (and when we write shortly, we mean only from a geological perspective which measures time in millions of years) this single continent began to break up into two separate parts. The northern one is called Laurasia and encompasses, after further splitting; into Europe, Asia, and North America. The other one, to the south, designated as Gondwanaland, includes the rest of the continents: Africa, South America, the Antarctic, and what is important for us, Australia, as the future parent-continent of New Guinea.

The breakup of Pangea

By the time of the breakup of Pangea, life on Earth had evolved into primitive plants like gymnosperms, plants with naked or unprotected seeds, such as conifers and cycads. Animal life was characterized by fishes, amphibians and the earliest of mammals but reptiles ruled the land. Primitive birds, evolving from reptiles, also appeared at this time. Any plant or animal life form existing before the breakup of Pangea could disperse relatively easily over the entire surface of the Earth, but once the splitting of the landmass began this was no longer possible. Evolution proceeded at its slow pace, but could follow separate paths and produce different life forms. To be sure, some of these life forms could cross water barriers, but others could not and became isolated in their water-bound geographical area. We will cover the evolution of plant and animal life that led to today's flora and fauna in the next chapter on the biodiversity in West New Guinea.

By some 150 million years ago, the splitting of Pangea was well on its way, with the Tethys Ocean separating most of the two landmasses. A small, incipient body of water to become the Atlantic Ocean, was just beginning to interpose itself between the southwestern part of Pangea (destined to become North America and Europe) and the northwestern part of Gondwanaland, the future South America, Australia and Africa. Towards the east, the landmass that was to become Southeast Asia and China were already far to the north from the eastern reaches of Gondwanaland.

During the Cretaceous period, which lasted from 145 to 65 million years ago, continents slowly drifted further and further apart. This long time span witnessed the appearance of grasses and cereals, the angiosperms (flowering plants characterized by enclosed seeds) in the flora, along with fauna of small, primitive mammals and the great dinosaurs. At the end of this period, the dinosaurs died out, along with many other invertebrate animal groups.

New Guinea emerges

We saw earlier that Australia was the far-eastern end of Gondwanaland while Southeast Asia-to-be was located at the far eastern end of Laurasia. These two landmasses were destined to be eventually connected by a great archipelago, present-day Indonesia. But first, the two landmasses had to approach each other. Southeast Asia moved a relatively short distance towards the equator while Australia came up a long ways from its far-south position towards the north. The leading northern edge of Australia eventually became New Guinea. However, during the long drift to the north, the forward edge of Australia spent considerable time underwater, sometimes connected to Australia, sometimes as separate islands. Bits and pieces of Australia's northern coastline had broken off at various times during its northward progress, submerging and emerging as islands from the ocean surface. These were the bits which would eventually coalesce to form the bulk of New Guinea.

All of the planet's major landmasses ride on huge platforms called tectonic plates, bodies of land 'floating' on top of the earth's molten interior. Some hardly move. Others have drastically shifted their position on the surface of the earth. These may move slowly by human standards, but nothing can stop them—except another tectonic plate. When two of these plates meet, they crunch against each other and you can be sure of fireworks: volcanic explosions, earthquakes and lots of upheavals. This is how New Guinea's mountains were formed.

After its long, leisurely and unimpeded move northward, Australia became much more interesting in the Middle Miocene period, some 15 million years ago. By then it had come in contact with the huge Pacific Plate, as well as the arc of the Indonesian islands, the southern edge of the archipelago. Push came to shove on a massive scale as the Australian and Pacific tectonic plates crunched together. This and many other forces working together have made New Guinea one of the most complex geological areas in the world: the leading edge of the Australian continental plate (called the Sahul Shelf) crunching with other plates and an inner and outer series of island arcs. Their structure can now be seen in New Guinea's two parallel mountain systems, the north and the central one. What is now New Guinea, riding on the northern margin of the Australian plate, collided with southward migrating volcanic arcs that stuck to our island.

This geological history is responsible for having created today's Papuan geography. New Guinea, covering almost 800,000 square kilometers, is the second largest island in the world, after Greenland. It is slightly bigger than the third contender, Borneo (Kalimantan). The Indonesian half of New Guinea makes up a whopping 22 per cent of the nation's total land area—yet holds only about one per cent of the country's population.

The highlands of the central mountain range

A 2000-kilometer-long mountain range, which runs most of the east-west length of the island (a total of about 2400 kilometers), represents the island's most remarkable feature. The mountain crests reach 3000 meters, with a handful of rocky peaks soaring above 4500 meters. The island's highest peak, Nemangkawi (or Puncak Jaya) tops out at 4884 meters. Its base is graced by the only remaining glaciers found on the island, the rest having melted due to the recent warming of the earth's temperature. This peak is the highest elevation between the Himalayas and the Andes. The young age of these geologically recent mountains is evident by the steep slopes, which have not yet been worn down by wind, water and rain erosion. The mountain mass consists largely of sedimentary limestones, sandstones and shale, uplifted from the former ocean bottom. The mountain range traces the exact line where the Sahul/Australian Plate and the Pacific Plate met.

The highlands of West New Guinea extend some 600 kilometers on a broadly east-west axis. The western end of this area lies just beyond (west) of the Paniai Lakes while the easternmost extreme stops abruptly at the international border with the independent nation of Papua New Guinea. Of course, neither geography nor culture stop at the border: the Ok and other ethnic groups straddle the international boundary while the mountains-and-valleys geography continues through the highlands of Papua New Guinea for approximately the same distance as in West New Guinea.

Volcanic action, more evident in the eastern part of New Guinea, has also left traces, in the form of igneous rock in West New Guinea. The best known of these has become the Grasberg Mine, now excavated into a huge hole by Freeport Indonesia for its copper and gold contents. The central mountain range is divided into several large chunks, with the Wisnumurti Range at the Papuan New Guinea border heading west, adjacent and contiguous with the Jayawijaya Range in the center and the Sudirman Range to the far western end of the mountains, at the Paniai Lakes. Some maps still show the Dutch names for these ranges: the Star Mountains to the east, the Oranje Mountains in the center and the Nassau Mountains to the west. In the Wisnumurti Range, we find the highest peak Gunung Mandala (formerly Mt. Juliana) at 4700 meters while Gunung Trikora (formerly Mt. Wilhelmina) at 4743 meters tops the Jayawijaya Range. We have seen that the highest peak of all, Nemangkawi (the local Amungme name for Puncak Jaya) reaches 4884 meters. It was not climbed to its summit until 1962. On most maps, this highest of peaks was originally called Carstensz Top but after the integration of West New Guinea with Indonesia, the name was officially changed to Puncak Jayakesuma, usually shortened to Puncak Jaya. We think that the best name for this high peak should be Nemangkawi Ninggok, which means 'the peak/tip of the white arrow'. This is from the language of the Amungme, the landowners whose territory holds this mountain.

The highlands of the central part of West New Guinea fall sharply to the south but only gradually to the north. This is because the mass of the Pacific Plate, located to the north, pushed up the leading edge of the Sahul or Australian plate, which crunched into it from the south. Most of the human concentration of the highlands lies above 700 meters but below 2400 meters. The densely wooded lower mountain slopes sharply in the south to the lowlands and the coastal swamps, while in the north the decline is more gradual, to a huge flat area called the Meervlakte, Dutch for the Lakes Plain of the Mamberamo Basin. This vast area is flat, swampy, full of Nipa palms and lowland forest, very thinly populated and little explored. The lack of any steepness in the area results in slowly meandering snake-shaped rivers. There are two main ones, the Taritatu (formerly the Idenburg) flowing from the east and the Tariku (formerly the Rouffaer) flowing from the west towards the center of the vast plain. They unite to become the Mamberamo at the middle of the Lakes Plain, and flow to the sea to the north. Gaps in the southern mountain range allow rivers to flow to the south, to the Arafura Sea.

The furthest western extension of the mountains reaches the Arafura Sea near Etna Bay. From there to the east and to the west, the coastal plain widens quite gradually, leaving room for various major groups of Papuans, starting with the Kamoro in the west, followed by the Asmat, and finally to the Marind-anim towards Merauke. In the southeast corner of West New Guinea, the prevalent coastal mangrove swamp gives way to an unusual area of dry, grassy savannah, where introduced deer are now abundant, along with native wallabies. This ecological zone is quite different from any other in New Guinea, more like Africa or Australia than a tropical island coast.

The Bird's Head

At the far western end of West New Guinea, a large appendage, almost a separate island, takes its name, the Bird's Head, from what might look to imaginative folks as the overall shape of New Guinea: a squatting bird sitting on its tucked-under legs. The 'head' of New Guinea detaches very clearly (on the map) from the rest of the body with Bintuni Bay cutting almost all the way across the island from the Banda Sea to Cenderawasih Bay. This bay hosts the most extensive mangrove swamp in the world, along with huge reserves of natural gas. The Bird's Head itself produces petroleum, albeit in moderate quantities.

The vegetation of the Bird's Head tends to lowland forest in the south, then less lush growth to the north marked by the Tamrau Mountains in the center and the Arfak Mountains inland from Manokwari. Parts of this landscape show karst formation, where the tropical climate eroded the basic limestone into fantastically shaped spires and gorges. These features make overland travel almost impossible.

The lowlands of New Guinea can boast of endless multi-hued butterflies, with fantastic (and useful) designs. The largest of the lot is the Goliath birdwing, **Ornithoptera goliath**, *with a 28 cm. wing span.*

BIODIVERSITY 2

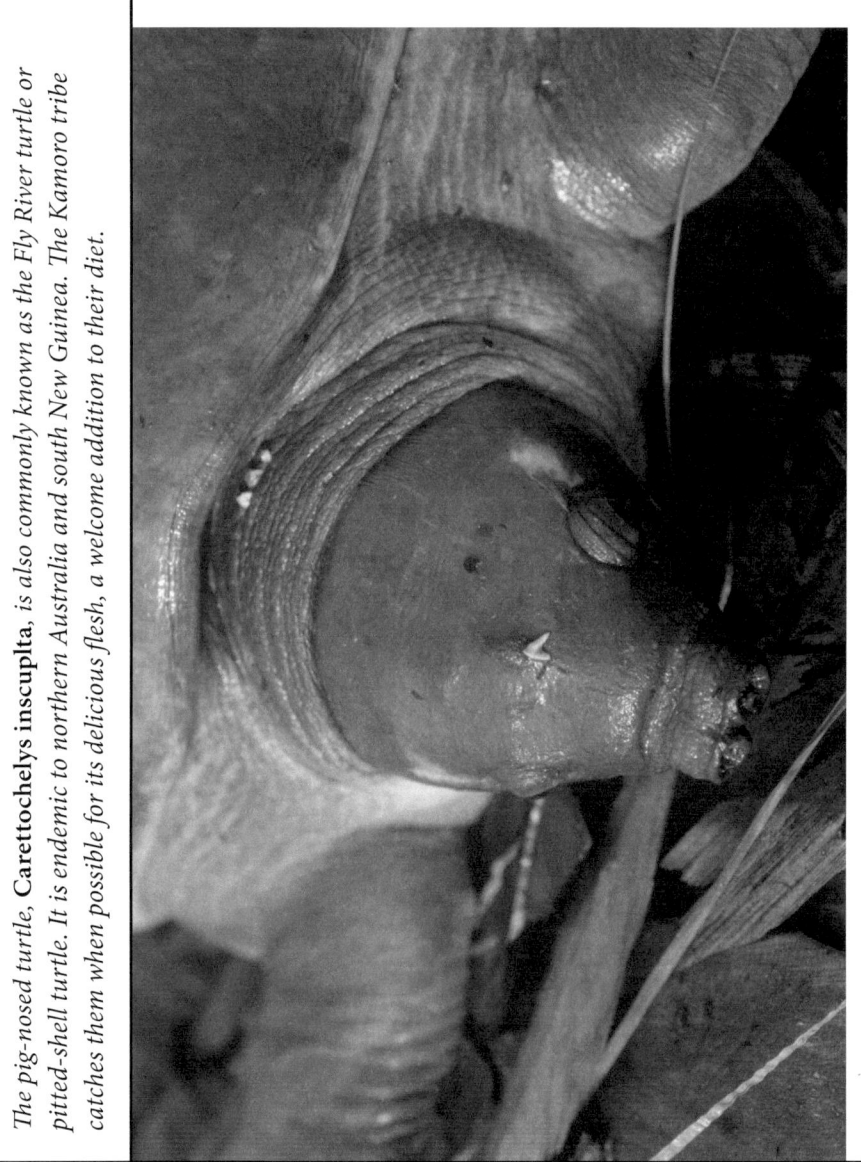

*The pig-nosed turtle, **Carettochelys inscuplta**, is also commonly known as the Fly River turtle or pitted-shell turtle. It is endemic to northern Australia and south New Guinea. The Kamoro tribe catches them when possible for its delicious flesh, a welcome addition to their diet.*

New Guinea is a veritable treasure house of animal and plant diversity, much of which is found nowhere else on earth. While lowland flora and fauna have many similarities with the plants of Southeast Asia and the animals of Australia, the highlands concentrate a unique variety, which has evolved due to its isolation. This most unusual biodiversity represents an important part of the rich heritage of today's Papuans and must be preserved for future generations. This preservation is also a Papuan responsibility for the rest of the Indonesians as well as all humans, as it is a true world heritage.

An Englishman, named Alfred Wallace, was the first to recognize the uniqueness of Papuan (and eastern Indonesian) animals. As he traveled through this vast archipelago, he became aware of the marked difference between the types of animals in western Indonesia and those in the east. The crucial change occurs just east of Bali and Sulawesi, a demarcation, which became known as the Wallace Line used to mark the separation. To the west, we have the Asian biological region and to the east, the Australian one. The main difference between the two lies in the mammal's reproductive organs. To the west, we have placentals and to the east, the marsupials. Most of the world's 4,500-odd mammal species are placentals, with only about some 270 marsupials. These are mostly found in the Australian biological region (200), with some (70) also found in South America.

Placental means that the embryo, the fertilized egg of the female, develops within the placenta of the womb (or uterus) of the mother until birth when the baby is ready to face the world, albeit most still requiring various degrees of parental care. Marsupial means that the embryo stays a much shorter time inside the mother's body and at 'birth' crawls from inside the womb to an external pouch formed by the mother's skin. Most of the animals of this world are placentals and those found today in New Guinea, such as pigs and dogs, were introduced by humans. Bats and murids (rat-type animals) made it on their own from Southeast Asia, starting some 15 million years ago. The total number of mammals found on the island of New Guinea adds up to 225 at the last count, but more are still being discovered. Of these, 212 are indigenous and 13 introduced. Most mammals in New Guinea are either bats or murids (mice and rats). (Flannery, 1995)

*The coconut crab, **Birgus latro**, weighs in as the world's largest terrestrial arthropod, at just over 4 kg. It is found mostly on islands of the Indian Ocean and some of the Pacific ones. Due to its bountiful and delicious flesh, it has been extirpated from most of its habitats by humans, its only predators.*

Mammals

Mammals are distinguished from other animals by having body hair or fur and suckling their young. During the Age of the Dinosaurs, starting from 252 million years ago, mammals were small, shrew-like and mostly nocturnal to avoid being noticed (and gobbled up) by the large, dominant carnivorous reptiles. Their chance to rule the earth began only came some 65 million years ago, when the results of a large meteorite or comet hitting the earth created conditions that exterminated the dinosaurs, along with most other life forms. This great catastrophe however resulted in an evolutionary explosion of different mammal species, leading to the Age of the Mammals.

Mammals, however, started their evolutionary divergence long before the end of the dinosaurs. The first ones to break away from a common ancestor were the monotremes, or egg-laying mammals. This happened some 180 million years ago, when Pangea was just beginning to break up. The egg-laying feature of monotremes shows their closeness to the reptiles, as all mammals and all reptiles also had a common ancestor. There are only five surviving species of monotremes, and two of them are found in New Guinea. One, called the long-beaked echidna ('babi duri moncong panjang' or 'landak Irian'), known scientifically as *Zaglossus bruijnii*, is the largest contemporary monotreme. It can weigh up to 16 kg. but its large size makes the animals a target for hunters and only a few are left in highland areas where humans seldom venture. The other monotreme, a similar short-beaked echidna (the spiny anteater *Tachyglossus aculeatus*), is also found in Australia, the habitat of the other three species of monotremes.

Some 140 million years ago, the marsupials branched off the main line of mammals. Of the 200-odd species found in the Australian biological region, some 70 are present in New Guinea, including many endemics. For a long time, before the arrival of humans in New Guinea, they had few predators to fear. Now, their main defense against humans is the nocturnal habits of many species. The largest of the marsupials, the agile wallaby ('walabi tangkas') is the same animal as the typical larger leaping kangaroo of Australia. It is only found in the seasonally dry grasslands around Merauke. Other kinds of kangaroo live mostly in trees, a most unusual habitat for this type of animal. These animals, the tree-kangaroos of the genus *Dendrolagus*, are only found in New Guinea (six species) and northeastern Australia (two species).

There are two kinds of mammals as we have seen above: most are placentals. The females of the other kind of mammal, the marsupial, found in Australia,

New Guinea and in South America (with one lonely species in North America), do not have a placenta, but instead nurture their fetus in a pouch provided with teats for the mother's sustaining milk. Most of the endemic (indigenous, non-introduced) animals in New Guinea are marsupials, with many species found nowhere else, but distantly related to the marsupials of Australia.

Pigs have become of crucial importance to the highland cultures, yet there is no agreement among the experts as to just when these animals arrived in New Guinea. It could be that pigs were present in the highlands some 6,000 years ago, if the dates from a few pig bones found in rock shelters are accurate. We do know for certain that the pig (along with the dog and the chicken) arrived in New Guinea with a later group of migrants, the Austronesians (more on them later).

Crocodiles and their kin

Aside from the mammals, New Guinea is also well endowed with many other animals, some endemic, some also found in Australia, Asia or worldwide. There are two kinds of crocodiles in West New Guinea, with the smaller one (*Crocodylus novaeguinae*), living mostly further inland than the larger beast. The bigger species, called the estuarine crocodile (*Crocodylus porosus*), is still feared by coastal Papuans and claim occasional human victims. They can grow to a fearsome seven meters in length and aside from man (and parasites) have no natural enemies. These estuarine crocodiles are the most dangerous animals in New Guinea by far, aside from the malaria-bearing mosquitoes. A large crocodile once terrorized the Asmat village of Piramat until it was finally killed in 1970: the monster was said to be seven meters long and was known to have taken 55 human victims along with countless dogs during its reign. But since their skins are valuable, hunters have now taken so many crocodiles that they are protected from hunting by non-Papuans or they would soon become extinct. Some coastal Papuans still hunt them at night for their flesh and the animals have learned to stay away from humans. But on isolated rivers and estuaries, they can still be seen on the banks, quickly slipping into water at the sight and sound of any boat with a motor.

The water monitor lizard (also mangrove monitor, mangrove goanna, Western Pacific monitor; *Varanus indicus*) is found in the same type of environment as the crocodile, and also extensively hunted by Papuans for its flesh. They are still quite abundant in many areas and are caught relatively easily. On the south coast of West New Guinea their skins are stretched taut into becoming the playing surfaces of drums. Many different species of frogs also serve as food for Papuans, especially in the mountains where larger animals have been hunted to near-extinction. Along with insects, frogs serve as an important source of protein for women and children in the highlands. There are more frog species on the island of New Guinea than anywhere else of comparable size. Many new endemic ones have been recently discovered. Some hardy species can live at elevations of over 3800 meters!

Essential fish life

Fish life in and around West New Guinea shows great diversity. There are probably some 3000 fish species in the sea off the coast of the island, abundant enough for commercial operations as well as providing the most important source of protein for the groups living along the coasts. This abundant (and tasty!) food source, along with sago, makes up the staple diet of many Papuans. Freshwater fishes are less important as a food source, and no native species (except for a single species, the Paniai gudgeon, *Oxyeleotris wisselensis*) exist in the highland, although during the recent past some outside species have been introduced into the Baliem River and elsewhere.

Up to quite recently, two freshwater lakes in West New Guinea could boast of the most unusual inhabitants. Lake Yamur hosted freshwater sharks, found almost nowhere else and Lake Sentani was home to large sawfish, up to 5 meters in length. Unfortunately, the sharks are no longer found in Yamur, probably since the local Papuans living along its shores started using nets to catch them. The sawfish of Lake Sentani were long protected by the belief and that ancestral spirits lived in them and thus its meat was taboo to the shore dwellers. But it has been a long time since one has been seen, so they are also probably extinct in the lake. Far from being extinct, we have some 158 species of small, colorful rainbow fishes, many endemic to West New Guinea. These unique animals are much in demand by aquarists, along with the small, also colorful reef fishes.

Birds-of-paradise

The variety of bird life is colorful and abundant in West New Guinea. Of course, the most famous of them, the birds-of-paradise, can be considered the symbol of the whole island. Of the 42 known species, 36 are found in New Guinea and its nearby islands. (Australia and Seram Island hold the remaining six species.) Few people, including Papuans, have seen these birds in the wild. They are shy, and for good reason: their magnificent feathers are much in demand. Fortunately, this demand has decreased considerably since it is no longer fashionable to wear them by ladies in the rich countries. But they still adorn some spectacular headdresses of Papuans. The most common, the Greater Bird of Paradise, has a long history of adorning the powerful rulers of countries like Nepal and Turkey with their bright yellow plumages, although, occasionally, feathers from other species appeared. Some of these feathers are absolutely mind-boggling—long, paired ones coming out places which have no business bearing them: out of the head or throat of some of these birds. One of the species, the Wilson's Bird of Paradise, shows off a blue head, yellow upper back, red lower back and green chest, plus a pair of elegantly curled tail feathers. How can any female resist his advances? The King of Saxony Bird of Paradise sports a pair of feathers sprouting from the back of its head, each feather measuring over twice the body length of this show-off. Another one has a pair of tail feathers over four times its body length. And the list of wonderfully unusual colors and plumages goes on and on.

For many years after the skin and plumes from the Greater Bird of Paradise were taken to Europe and created a scientific stir: the animal had no legs! Learned men came up with stories to justify this zoological freak of nature: the bird had no need of feet as it flew continuously until it died. The female laid her eggs on the back of the male and incubated them right there as well, as the poor chap kept flying and flying. Even the scientific name of this bird reflects this gross error: *Paradisea apoda*, which is Latin for 'legless bird-of-paradise'. It was too late to correct the error when Europeans found out the truth of the matter: the Papuans who prepared the skins of these birds for trade or sale simply cut off the feet for convenience, as it was only the feathers that were valuable!

Other unusual birds include the fierce but much hunted cassowary, with claws that can disembowel a human. These flightless birds are usually stalked with dogs and killed with spears or arrows so the hunter can remain a safe distance away. Their plentiful flesh is consumed (after much cooking as it is too tough otherwise), and the feathers used in headdresses and other body decorations. Easier to hunt and with much more delectable flesh, we have crown pigeons ('mambruk'), and the megapods who bury their eggs which then hatch by the natural heat of the heaped mounds built by the parents.

The bowerbirds, quite plain when compared to the birds-of-paradise, make up for this by building ground-level displays to attract discriminating females. These displays, called bowers, are made up of twigs and decorated with all kinds of neatly lined up colorful objects from flowers to berries, to items filched from humans such as twine or bits of cloth. The females walk around inspecting these bowers and then mate with the builder of the one they esteem as the most ingeniously decorative and colorful. The female then makes her own plain nest and concentrates on the essential task of mothering the chicks.

Many insects, some useful, others not

Insects represent an important food source to many Papuans. In the highlands, women and children supplement their diet and eat many species, an important source of protein, including the larvae. On the coast, especially in the south, the sago grub has long been an important source of fat and supplementary protein as well. The sago tree is cut down and left to rot, attracting a special kind of beetle that lay its eggs in the starch-rich pith of the trunk. After some three to five weeks, the grubs are harvested and consumed. The Kamoro eat the grubs raw, roasted or mostly cooked with sago. The Asmat have developed an elaborate ritual requiring huge quantities of these grubs.

With some 100,000 insect species, West New Guinea can again boast of an extremely diverse and interesting range of life forms. There are more beetles than any other species, serving as food as well as body decorations. Spiders are numerous, with about 800 species, led by their king, the formidable bird-eating giant, (scientifically known as *Selenocosmia crassides*) which reverses the usual order of hunter and prey species. Some insects are pests, such as mosquitoes and flies, but most serve mankind by performing functions essential in maintaining the various eco-systems.

Most distinctive and colorfully beautiful; the numerous contingents of butterflies are dominated by the gigantic species, the birdwings. While these can be found in many places, the greatest concentration and diversity lies in the Arfak Mountains, just inland from Manokwari. The shimmering hues of the wings have long captivated outsiders, and there is a good potential for raising these beauties for local sale as well as export. The largest one, appropriately named the Goliath birdwing (*Ornithoptera goliath*) can reach 28 centimeters, wingtip to wingtip.

Mollusks

Coastal Papuans consume a wide variety of mollusks that includes a number of endemics. The Kamoro of the south coast feast on one particular species that they consider a gastronomic delicacy.

Aficionados only eat it raw, best just pulled out of its self-dug labyrinth inside a tree trunk where it has developed a long, soft, naked body. A pair of raspers makes up the front of the beast, used to bore into wood and pass the 'sawdust' into its digestive tract. It is usually called 'tambelo' in Indonesian, locally named '*pa'a*'. Scientifically known as *Batronophorus thoracites*, this worm-like creature is really a bivalve mollusk. The two shells that make it a bivalve do not protect the body, as with oysters and clams but have evolved into rasping appendages. These allow the 'tambelo' to bore its way into fallen mangrove trees of the genus *Rhizophora*. This refined Kamoro tidbit belongs to the *Teredinida* family, better known as the destructive shipworms, the termites of the sea that chew up wooden boats, docks and timber pilings. It tastes like a sweet oyster. Delicate souls might want to marinate the 'tambelo' in lime juice and a bit of Tabasco sauce prior to ingestion.

Plant life

As with the animals, the plant life of West New Guinea is the greatest and most diverse of any other area in Indonesia. While the lowland rainforest is quite similar to that of northern Queensland in Australia, and that of Southeast Asia, the highlands concentrate the many unique species found only on this island. Botanists estimate the number of plant species at about 16,000. Many are valuable for local medicines, which potentially could have components useful to modern drugs. Unfortunately, the lowlands rainforest also holds valuable and accessible hardwood timber, now being cut down at a rate that is not sustainable, as these trees take many, many years to grow back again.

Some 3,000 species of orchids have been found on New Guinea, with many of them in the highlands unique to this island. Some other unusual botanical wonders include the giant ant-house plants found in the highlands, growing protruding from trees. They are filled with passageways teeming with ants and even small frogs have been found inside. Pitcher plants, growing in nitrogen-poor soils, eat insects to fulfill this requirement by forming slippery cups of liquid nectar, which trap and digest insects.

Aside from the valuable hardwood timbers, the lowland swamps in many areas are filled with sago trees. The pith of these trees turns edible just before flowering. After the trees are cut down, the pith is broken up with a special adze, mixed with water and passed through a sieve to separate the woody cellulose strands from the pure starch. Sago is the staple food for most coastal dwellers even today, although a number who can afford it have come to prefer rice. While making sago is very labor-intensive, a few days of work by a family can produce enough carbohydrate to last for a month. It is one of the few locally produced foods that can keep without refrigeration.

With such a rich biodiversity, West New Guinea must make a great effort to conserve these wonders for its future first of all, but also for all mankind. It is truly a world-heritage site but often, local greedy politicians, the military and outside commercial interests are unwilling to practice sustainable exploitation of the natural resources. These practices must be stopped at any cost!

An Amungme elder in the highlands of central West New Guinea. He was participating in a large-scale traditional ritual that included killing many pigs for he ancestral spirits.

MIGRATION FROM AFRICA TO NEW GUINEA

3

An Asmat man living in the lowland swamps wears a cuscus fur hat and a dogs' teeth necklace. The Asmat were the last important group to submit to Dutch colonial control, in the mid-1950s.

The earliest ancestors of today's Papuans arrived on the island of New Guinea at least 50,000 years ago. They came from Africa, as did all modern humans. Some pre-modern humans left Africa earlier (groups arrived in Java, China and elsewhere about two million years ago) but over time they became extinct.

The facts of evolution tell us that all life forms found today on our planet evolved over some 4 billion years from the simplest life. Common ancestors begot descendants which evolved in different ways, resulting in almost countless species which became extinct, but include all of today's variety of life as well. All of today's humans have a common ancestor, who lived in Africa over five or six million years ago. This same ancestor also begot the chimpanzees. Adapting to the changing physical environment, essentially due to changes of climate, led to the divergent evolution of the bodies of the humans and chimpanzees. Humans gradually evolved to walk upright, with ever-larger brains, the ability to control fire and use tools. And, lastly but a crucially important development was the ability to use complex, expressive, and grammatical language. What are called 'modern' humans, people whose physical and mental features are similar to ours, 'appeared' some 200,000 years ago in Africa.

We know that some pre-modern humans had migrated out of Africa. Then, much later, some groups of modern humans also left Africa for Europe, Asia and elsewhere. The ancestors of today's Papuans traveled close to the shoreline of what is now the Arabian Peninsula, and then along the northern shores of the Indian Ocean. Some of these people did not make it as far as New Guinea, but it may be that a number of their descendants are surviving to this day in southern India, the Andaman Islands, Malaysia and the Philippines. At that time, the ancestors of the bulk of today's Southeast Asian population had not yet arrived in these areas. We do not know if there were any survivors of the early migration in western parts of the country, when the present-day ancestors of today's majority of Indonesians first arrived about 5,000 years ago.

So the ancestors of today's Papuans left Africa, and eventually ended up in Australia as well as New Guinea. We can only speculate as to the reasons why these people left Africa. Perhaps with climatic changes, they could no longer sustain themselves. Perhaps population pressures had a role. But for whatever reasons, they did leave Africa, the cradle of humanity, and headed towards the unknown.

We must not think of this migration as one with masses of people moving together with any sort of coordination. Rather, it was very probably a series of small-scale groups on the move, for hundreds if not thousands of years. It is likely that they found sustenance along the coasts they followed by gathering various types of mollusks and other shore animals. Perhaps they fished as well. They probably experimented with attempting to eat what they found in the surrounding vegetation, but they relied on the known seashore foods. Eventually, they reached Malaysia and made their way along land and water through what is now the Indonesian chain of islands. While with the then lower sea levels they could easily make their way overland as far as Bali, but from there on they had to master the art of water navigation to travel any further.

Even when the sea level was at its lowest due to the Ice Ages, these brave and adventurous pioneers had to cross some long stretches of seas that separated them from their then-unknown final destination, Australia and New Guinea. It is most likely that they crossed open seas on wooden or bamboo rafts able to carry at least five people, the minimum viable colonizing population. This was a feat of long-distance sea crossing which no other humans attempted for many millennia afterwards. These Papuan ancestors were at the leading edge of the technology of the day, far ahead of any other human groups. No other humans undertook sea voyages like that for a long, long time, showing the advanced state of Papuan navigation. Within the sheltered confines of the Mediterranean Sea, sea voyages like those undertaken by Papuans did not happen until some 10,000 years ago.

We have archeological proof of the early arrival of these sea-borne pioneers. The earliest known site of human occupation is located on the Huon Gulf terraces on the north coast of Papua New Guinea. Papuans settled there some 50,000 to 60,000 years ago. Excavations there also yielded stone axes, called 'waisted' due to a groove that was made for a more secure attachment to the handle.

Nor did these pioneer navigators stop once they settled on New Guinea. They went on to some other islands to the north and east, crossing stretches as long as over 200 kilometers (to reach Manus Island). This took place at least 13,000 years ago. Another epic sea voyage by Papuans took place much earlier, reaching Buka Island in the northern Solomons at least 29,000 years ago.

Papuan pioneers in New Guinea

When they finally arrived on the island of New Guinea, Papuans first settled on the shores where they could continue eating shellfish and other familiar foodstuffs. These were initially gastropods (animals with a single, spiral shell), such as Turbos and Nerites and later more bivalves (animals with two identical shells held together with a hinge), resembling clams, such as *Geloina coaxans*, whose shells are useful scrappers. These shellfish are still consumed along the coasts of West New Guinea. The pioneer ancestors also hunted marsupials that at first had no fear of humans. They also very likely captured and ate monitor lizards, of the common and widespread species, *Varanus indicus* being then (and now) an important source of protein, as its adults weigh two to four kilos. These lizards can grow to over 1.2 meters, and their skins can now (and perhaps in the distant past as well) be extensively used as the playing surface of hourglass-shaped drums. The early Papuans also found several species of larger marsupial land animals but these have now became extinct, probably due to over-hunting.

During the colder climates of the Ice Ages, with the sea levels being lower, there was more exposed shoreline for early Papuans to exploit for food resources. With the warming of the earth's weather, the Arafura Sea rose to perhaps a meter or more above present levels. Later the surface settled down to its current tidemarks some 6,000 years ago. This movement led to today's extensive mangrove swamps, a rich food resource for those who know what to look for and when: for many coastal dwellers, the mangrove swamps represent a huge, free supermarket. The opening and closing hours change daily with the tides.

Some early Papuans probably made their way inland to hunt but it is unlikely that they stayed very long until much later. The permanent, large-scale settlement of New Guinea's highlands had to wait for the weather to change. The areas where today we find the major population concentrations, the fertile valleys, were not welcoming to humans for a long time. The climate was cooler and drier then. From 30,000 to 10,000 years ago, glaciers covered large inland areas of New Guinea Island (glaciers were the most extensive 18,000 years ago) and the tree line was considerably (up to 1700 meters) below today's level of some 3900 meters. This crucial tree line, a major factor in determining animal life, fluctuated with temperature changes. Dominant southern beech trees (*Nothofagus*) were widespread, and, when the climate allowed, reached from 1500 meters elevation, up to as high as 2100 meters. This type of tree, then as today, thrives on persistent cloudiness and mist, conditions that only favor a restricted range of other types of vegetation.

When the worst of the cold climate, which lasted from 20,000 to 15,000 years ago, was over, the temperature rose accordingly. This allowed for many complex changes in the vegetation. And the most important difference for humans perhaps, was the freeing of the main highland valleys from their cloud and mist climate, leading to diversification of the existing forest, as well as the rising tree line. By around 10,000 to 9,000 years ago, the inland climate became quite similar to that existing today. The human ancestors of today's highland populations took advantage of this welcoming climate.

As the world's climate warmed, a few small groups did begin to make their way inland to live there permanently. The retreating glaciers allowed forests to expand into higher elevations, with game animals following the vegetation. Thus, the earliest Papuans to make their way inland were hunters, as well as gatherers, finding by experiment what was edible from their environment. For several millennia, only small groups were able to survive in the highlands, as game was not plentiful. At that time, pigs had not yet made their way to New Guinea, thus after the extinction of larger mammals, hunting was restricted to smaller game, almost exclusively indigenous marsupials, along with birds and rats.

At this time, the lifestyle of the highland pioneers began to change. It is not possible to make a clear and simple distinction between hunter-gatherers and agriculturists. The change was more like a very gradual one, with foraging slowly losing its primordial importance. With the warming climate changes, some plant species died off as the rainforest species climbed up and returned to the higher mountains slopes.

The earliest evidence we have of agricultural activity comes from a highland swamp called Kuk in Papua New Guinea. This dates back to 9,000 years ago and ranks among humans' earliest cultivation, an independent center of plant domestication. The swamp was partially drained to encourage the growth of taro (*Colocasia esculenta*), probably derived from a wild type, which had little starch but edible shoots and leaves. The selection by Papuans of those plants for starch contents of the underground tuber occurred during the early phases of cultivation.

Located at the entrance of the huge Cenderawasih Bay, Biak Island lies at the edge of the Pacific Ocean. The island was the site of a fierce battle—Operation Hurricane—between Japanese and US forces during World War II.

4

MIGRATION FROM ASIA: THE AUSTRONESIANS BECOME MELANESIANS (LAPITA CULTURE)

This young girl from Biak holds her mixed heritage from early Papuans, as well as much later arrivals from Taiwan, called Malayo-Polynesians.

We are now ready to meet another group of New Guinean, known in the literature as '*Austronesians*,' and are often abbreviated by the capital letters '*AN*'. In keeping with this designation, the original inhabitants of New Guinea are awkwardly called non-Austronesians, abbreviated to NAN.

This term 'Austronesian', a language designation, can create confusion as it is close to 'Australian' but has nothing to do with the aborigines of Australia who arrived long before this new group. The Austronesians originated from China, migrated to Taiwan some 6,000 years ago and then spread to the south. Once out of Taiwan, these people are called 'Malayo-Polynesians', a term much easier to understand: Malays and Polynesians (as a unit). This group of hardy sailors became today's most widespread linguistic group, covering most of the area between Easter Island in the east, and Madagascar Island to the west, just off the coast of Africa. Theirs was an on-going expansion lasting many centuries. In fact, the first inhabitants of Madagascar reached their new homeland from south Kalimantan (Indonesian Borneo) only some 1,500 years ago. Aside from its wide geographical reach, covering some two-thirds of the circumference of the world near the equator, the Austronesian language family makes up some one sixth of today's languages. There are some 5,000 languages still spoken in the world. While the Austronesian languages make up about one sixth, the languages spoken in New Guinea Island (Papuan—or NAN—as well as Austronesian—or AN-languages) make up one fifth, concentrated in a far smaller geographical area.

So, long after the pioneer inhabitants of New Guinea, a second group of ancestors arrived, the Austronesian. Leaving Taiwan some 5,000 years ago, they began to spread south, thanks to two crucial inventions: the outrigger canoe and the sail. Here again, there was no mass exodus. Small groups first reached the northern Philippines, worked their way south, then split along two major directions. Some headed southwest, to the island of Borneo (Kalimantan), and then to Malaysia, Sumatra and Java. They were the ancestors of most of today's Malays and western Indonesians. The other group headed southeast, to Halmahera, to the northern coast of New Guinea and, especially to the islands of the Bismarck Archipelago. From there, they settled in the Solomon Islands, Vanuatu, and New Caledonia, Fiji and then further to the east to eventually populate Polynesia. This was made possible only by their advanced water navigation and sailing techniques.

The Austronesians in New Guinea

For several good reasons the Austronesians decided to settle for a while, in the Bismarck archipelago, starting around 4,000 years ago, before moving into the vast reaches of the Pacific Ocean. This archipelago is made up of many small islands, a middle-sized one called Manus, long but thin New Ireland and the by far the largest, New Britain. The islands are volcanic, with ancient and recent large-scale devastating eruptions on New Britain. But volcanic activity has a positive side as well: once the ash from an explosion settles down, it makes the land very fertile (as also evidenced in Java). Volcanic activity also produces obsidian, a black glass-like stone that can be chipped or split to a sharp cutting edge, a most useful tool and a prized trade item.

The original Papuan inhabitants of New Guinea had reached most major and minor islands located relatively close to the mainland before the arrival of the Austronesian. These islands included New Britain, New Ireland and much of the Solomons, all prior to 10,000 years ago. And sometimes much earlier: 30,000 years ago for the northern Solomons. But they did not venture any further, probably due to the wide expanses of the seas to the next but distant groups of islands, Vanuatu and Fiji. The Austronesian newcomers eventually did travel there, and much further, populating the islands in the vast expanses of the central and eastern Pacific Ocean.

The Austronesian (AN) group of people stopped in the Bismarck Archipelago and most likely on other islands such as Biak and Yapen. This is supported by linguistic evidence but not yet by archeology for West New Guinea, as systematic scientific excavations have not begun. It is most likely that where the newcomers did settle, they integrated with the existing local Papuan groups. These were probably quite small bands of hunter-fisher-gatherers, with some practicing horticulture.

With larger groups of people already on the mainland of New Guinea, it was probably more difficult for the Austronesians to settle down permanently. It seems that these newcomer (AN) settlements on the north shore of New Guinea happened only some 1,000 years after their establishment in the Bismarcks. But with scant archeological work along this coast, experts can only conjecture and make educated guesses about this.

The new arrivals in the Bismarcks developed a particular culture that has become known as Lapita. This name comes from a site in New Caledonia where the type of fine pottery, which characterizes this culture, was first found and identified. This reddish pottery was decorated with small teeth-like (dentate) designs with some of these highlighted using a contrasting white made of clay or lime. Lapita-style pottery has been found from the Bismarcks all the way to Polynesia, along with the dispersal of languages from the same AN family.

The Austronesians were a technologically advanced culture, with domesticated animals (including chickens, dogs and the essential pig), a range of useful imported plants, better tools and a structured social organization with a hierarchy, probably with hereditary chiefs. They also produced a complex set of shell ornaments and implements, including fishhooks, armbands, and trumpets. The Austronesians from New Britain extended the existing—but short distance—trade in volcanic obsidian from New Britain to an area from present-day Sabah in northern Borneo all the way to Fiji.

The new arrivals integrated with existing early Papuan populations who, while only present in small groups, had overcome the natural limits of their forest environment and had taken an active part in shaping it for their benefit. However, they ran into a major problem, which persists to this day: malaria. As with today's coastal and lowland groups (living up to around 1500 meters' elevation) malaria can be devastating. However, if the most vulnerable group, the small children, can survive the malaria attacks to the age of five years, they acquire a degree of immunity, which at least partially protects them into adulthood. However, this immunity can vanish with new arrivals, such as today's transmigrant Javanese and Bugis moving to West New Guinea. The non-immune migrants are very susceptible to malaria and cause a rapid expansion of the parasite leading to epidemics (unless controlled by modern medical care). The increased number of malarial parasites overcomes the locals' partial immunity, especially for the most vulnerable: the children and pregnant women. Not having access to modern medicine, the Austronesian, without understanding what causes malaria, were able to survive the disease by their lifestyle: villages of stilt-perched houses built over lagoons or on small offshore islands, thus avoiding land-based malarial mosquitoes. The normal range of mosquitoes is about a half a kilometer from their stagnant-water breeding grounds, although winds can blow them considerably further. But if the human settlements are over a half-kilometer away, the chances of being stung decrease considerably.

We have seen that the Austronesian/Lapita culture possessed several technological advances which eventually allowed them to travel to the furthest islands of the Pacific: excellent long-range sailing craft, navigational techniques, a high degree of organization, world-class tools and undoubtedly a spirit of adventure. But, there was a key element that combined with the above which allowed them to reach and survive in the remote islands of the Pacific: efficient-scale agriculture, with improved techniques. This was crucial as the native fauna (as well as flora) in the islands became increasingly reduced the further one traveled from mainland New Guinea. It would have been impossible for any group to survive for long while only practicing hunting and gathering. The ecology was insufficient to provide for that lifestyle. In order to settle these islands known today as Vanuatu, New Caledonia, Fiji and beyond, well-developed agriculture was essential.

A vexing question: the timing of the pigs' first arrival

We all know how important pigs are to New Guinea cultures. A Papuan once said to me in Indonesian: 'babi, sama masyarakat punya dompet', (pigs are the people's wallets or wealth) but it is more than just a source of affluence: in many areas, it remains an essential feature of the brideswealth, even in the modern era of cash-and-carry. While pig meat may not be used 'rationally' according to outsiders' standards, the large pig-killing feasts and pork-exchange were (and to a somewhat lesser extent, remain) an integral part of the highlands Papuan culture. Pigs turn surplus sweet potatoes into protein, and represent the essential animal resource, which has remained after over-hunting has drastically reduced the number of existing indigenous game.

The experts are in disagreement as to just when pigs first arrived in New Guinea. Was it with the Austronesians or before them? A few scientifically excavated sites in Papua New Guinea have revealed a very few pig bones dating back to pre-Austronesian times, but these findings have not gained universal acceptance. Everyone agrees however, that if there were pigs prior to the Austronesians, they were quite limited in numbers. There was perhaps a two-stage pig-arrival in New Guinea. One dating back to sometime over 6,000 years ago, thus before the arrival of the Austronesians, and then the later full-scale and rapid spread of these animals brought in as domesticates. Perhaps wild pigs made their own way across long stretches of the sea, or were brought by unknown immigrants who arrived much later than the Papuans but before the Austronesian. Or, perhaps the Papuans brought them in themselves in relatively recent times. We know that Papuan languages exist today in parts of Indonesia to the west of New Guinea: in Halmahera, Alor and Timor. So perhaps back-migration by Papuans brought them in contact with pigs in these areas. There are no satisfactory answers yet to the timing of the arrival of the first pigs to New Guinea. But most current research gives us no dates for pigs in New Guinea before 4,000 years ago.

What does Melanesia really mean?

We must pause here for some definitions of names, which can create confusion. The original inhabitants of New Guinea are generally called Papuans. They are also designated by linguists as the non-Austronesian (NAN) language family, due to a lack of a better term to encompass the near-incredible variety of their 750-odd languages in such a relatively small area. A different language family (and its speakers), called Austronesian (AN), is also present in Papua New Guinea and nearby islands, represented by some 150 different languages. These AN-designated folks are descendants of the second group of immigrants to New Guinea.

The meaning of the words Melanesia and Melanesians has evolved, changing with time.

The term 'Melanesia', literally meaning 'Black Islands' was first used by the French navigator, Dumont d'Urville in 1832. While exploring, the captain used the word for a geographical area, it was later taken up by others to designate a people with dark skin and tightly curled hair, in contrast with lighter-skinned, straight-haired Indonesians and Polynesians.

While showing a great deal of diversity, what has been called 'Melanesian' languages (more accurately designated as NAN) also show a degree of similarity, as do their economies, social organizations and religions which gave prime importance to various spirits, especially those of the recently deceased. For many years, before careful studies of the languages, Papuans as well as the Melanesians who lived on various islands (Solomons, Vanuatu, New Caledonia and Fiji) were covered by the umbrella of the Melanesian designation. (The Fijians, whose society was characterized by hereditary rank, were different in this respect from most of their fellow Melanesians.) The Australian aborigines, with black skins but wavy hair, were seldom if ever considered Melanesians.

The wide expanses of the Pacific have been divided into three major geographical regions. To the north, we have Micronesia, in the center and to the east, it's Polynesia and to the west, the designation is Melanesia. These names are from the Greek and Latin. The last part of each word is derived from 'nesos', meaning island. Then we have 'micro' meaning 'very small', 'poly' meaning 'many' and 'melano' meaning 'black'. (In the same way, Indo-nesia means 'islands of the Indies') Indeed, the islands of Micronesian are quite small, those of Polynesia are many and the inhabitants of Melanesia have black skins. Due to the meaning of this last name, many Papuans consider themselves Melanesians. However, the experts working with the languages and cultures of West New Guinea and Melanesia prefer to differentiate the two groups, applying the word Papuan (or non-Austronesian, NAN) to those descendants of the initial group of humans to arrive in New Guinea and reserving the term Melanesian (or, better, Austronesian, AN) for the late arrivals who speak a distinct and different group of languages and brought with them a different culture.

While the ancestors of the Austronesians originally had lighter skin color, their marriages with Papuans darkened the skins of their descendants and most of them today also have tightly curled hair, a Papuan/African characteristic. Some of their languages became mixed with Papuan ones. Yet genetic and linguistic differences between 'Papuans' and 'Austronesian-Melanesians' remain to this today. In the western half of New Guinea, Melanesians descendants predominate in the islands of Biak and Yapen, the Raja Ampat islands as well as in many pockets along stretches of the north coast. They are not found in the highlands, or along the south coast. It is interesting to note that Papuan languages are spoken in parts of Timor, Alor and Halmahera, perhaps due to either a westward migration by Papuans or ancestral groups who stayed in these islands at the time of the original Papuan migrations from the west.

There is no race that can be called 'Melanesian' (as separate from Papuan) in any genetic sense. Three thousand years of intermarriage and language shift have combined to negate differences. These well-established elements, combined with the fact that many Papuans consider themselves Melanesians, will allow us to use the term Melanesian in this book in the largest sense of the term: black-skinned. When we discuss linguistics (and pre-history), we will retain a differentiation, referring to Papuan languages as non-Austronesian (NAN) and the languages of the later migrants as Austronesian (AN).

A winning combination: the Melanesians

Long before the Austronesians' arrival, the Papuans had populated the islands off the north coast of New Guinea, islands such as Biak, Yapen, the Raja Ampat, New Ireland, New Britain and Bougainville. They had developed the use of obsidian, a volcanic, very tough, glass-like stone, which can be chipped to yield a sharp cutting edge: a most useful tool. They had also introduced mainland animals such as the common cuscus (*Phalanger orientalis*) to the islands as early as 20,000 years before Christ. Later, other animals were also taken to the islands including a bandicoot (*Echympera kalubu*). The Papuans also introduced various plants to these islands, including the important *Canarium* trees bearing galip nuts which can keep for up to three years.

We can say that the Melanesians are a relatively recent 'race', which genetically and culturally combined Papuans with the ancestors of the Indonesians and Polynesians. Each side brought benefits to the combined race. The Papuans, long masters of their environment, had developed agriculture, medium-distance trade (obsidian from New Britain) by sea to a distance of 350 kilometers, as well as the best possible use of the existing natural resources. The Austronesians brought with them better tools, pottery, domesticated animals such as dogs and chickens. This latter group also introduced better agricultural techniques, long-distance sea navigation (thanks to the outrigger and the sail), and long-distance trade.

The Austronesians who arrived in New Guinea settled on the offshore islands, perhaps because the mainland groups were larger and organized enough to be able to resist these Asian transmigrants. On the islands, the indigenous Papuans combined their genes and extensive local knowledge with the genes and culture of the newcomers. The combined 'new' race, the Melanesians, created a cultural complex now called Lapita.

Lapita pottery was first developed in the islands off New Guinea and then taken by the Melanesians as they expanded to the south and the east into the vast reaches of the Pacific Ocean. This expansion was made possible by two crucial factors: long-distance navigation and agriculture. The Vanuatu archipelago was the first group of islands reached by the Melanesians, a long ways over open seas from the Solomons Islands, the extreme limit of what had already been populated by the Papuans. To reach Vanuatu was impossible without ocean-going rafts or huge canoes. And once there, humans could not have survived long without agriculture due to a lack of edible wild plants such as yams or taro and decent sized animals. The poor natural resources of Vanuatu and other Pacific islands made for a barrier impenetrable to non-agricultural settlements.

The penetration of Melanesians into the Pacific is a long and fascinating story, but we will not follow it here as our focus is on the inhabitants of New Guinea.

The language factor

Papuan languages are so varied that there is no good word to designate them as a whole. The term Papuan itself is not really accurate, as some Papuans speak Malayo-Polynesian. The best term that linguists have come up with so far is the awkward Non-Austronesian (Non-Malayo-Polynesian). Remember that for New Guinea as a whole, we are dealing with a total of more than 1,000 languages, far more than in any comparable area in the world.

Linguists have analyzed the Austronesian (Malayo-Polynesian) languages from a historical point of view to tell us that they spread out of Taiwan some 5,000 years ago, then, after the Philippines, into Indonesia about 4,000 years ago, reaching New Guinea at least 3,500 years ago. Currently, there are some 150 Malayo-Polynesian languages spoken in New Guinea, almost all of them on offshore islands or along the north coast. All these languages have similarities in structure and vocabulary, which groups them into one language family. The rest of the languages now spoken in New Guinea, some 750 of them, present a far more difficult challenge to linguists attempting to group them into some sort of related units.

What methods do these experts use to find relationships to group languages into categories? There are two: the structure (grammar) and word similarities. For reasons best known to themselves, some linguists have decided that if two languages share 81% of their vocabulary, they are dialects of each other. If the shared words that amount to at least 28%, then the languages are of the same family. With the percentage dropping to 12 to 28%, they call the grouping the same 'stock'. And, finally, with the similarities in words ranging from 5 to 12%, languages belong to the same phylum.

In laymen's terms, we can say that mutually understandable languages are dialects of each other. However, science has to be more precise, whence the 81 per cent designation.

It is no easy task to make sense of the relationships (grammar and vocabulary) between some 750 non-Malayo Polynesian (NAN) languages. But brave linguists (led by a most erudite and dedicated man named Wurm) ventured to write that some 500 of New Guinea's languages could be grouped into a category called the Trans New Guinea Phylum. This represents about two-thirds of the total. The grouping includes some of the languages spoken in places as far away as Timor, Pantar and Alor. The languages that do not fit into this category are most of those spoken in the Bird's Head, the middle and lower reaches of the Sepik River and the lower parts of the Ramu River in Papua

New Guinea.

The possible connection between the development of root crop agriculture before 6,000 years ago and the dispersal of groups throughout the highlands is one possible reason given for the similarities found in the Trans New Guinea Phylum.

But if there are some similarities in this phylum group, there are great differences with other Papuan (non-Austronesian) languages. In fact, the differences between some groups of Papuan languages are as great as the differences with the most recent arrivals, the Austronesian ones.

Amungme men holding a pig carcass to a fire to singe off the bristles. All Amungme celebrations require killing pigs, the more, the better. The cooking takes place in underground ovens.

COASTAL AND HIGHLAND CONTRASTS

5

An open-fronted Korowai tree house dominates the surrounding jungle. A shield is displayed at the front. The high tree houses keep humans out of the reach of the malarial mosquitoes as well as keeping them safe from enemies.

The lifestyle of Papuans living on or near the coasts is quite unlike that of the highlanders. This is due almost exclusively to the contrasts in the environment (soil types, elevation and climate), which result in a different set of plants and animals to sustain human life.

With some exceptions along the north coast and offshore islands, the coastal Papuans tended to be hunters, fishermen and gatherers while the highland Papuans practiced agriculture as the main life-sustaining activity. The coastal Papuans main staple food, sago, is not traditionally cultivated and the processing of the sago trunks into something edible is a relatively simple process, which yields lots of calories for a relatively small amount of hard work. The mountain Papuans on the other hand need to devote much time and effort to raise their life-sustaining crops, with sweet potatoes as the main staple. While the men do the heavy initial task of clearing and fencing, it is the women who do most of the work in the sweet potato gardens.

Pigs and sweet potatoes

Sweet potatoes are a relatively recent introduction to the highlands, having only been cultivated there for the past few hundred years. It is a root crop, which comes from South America. Its cultivation allowed for a population explosion in the highlands with inhabitant concentrations far higher than in the coastal areas. Sweet potatoes yield more food per unit area of cultivation than taro; it can grow to higher elevations, and withstand colder temperatures. The original highlands staple, taro, retains a ritual importance and in some areas its cultivation was usually handled by men and not women, although this distinction is breaking down today. We will cover uplands agriculture more thoroughly in a another book devoted to the main highlands groups, from the Me tribe in the Paniai Lakes area to the Ok on the border with Papua New Guinea.

The raising of pigs is another major distinction between highlands and lowlands Papuans. While the coastal Papuans will raise an occasional captured piglet, this is not a major activity. On the other hand, the raising of domestic pigs is a crucial pursuit in the highlands where these animals still today represent the traditional source of wealth and, to some extent, power. They are still required in most areas as a major component of the bride price and for large-scale rituals where many are killed and the meat distributed to reinforce relationships and alliances.

While hunting and gathering were the major life-sustaining activities of the pioneer highlands Papuans, the former declined in importance with the advent of agriculture and the scarcity of game due to over-hunting. On the contrary, in many coastal areas, hunting is still practiced today (or until recently), with wild pigs, cassowaries, cuscus, tree kangaroos and other medium-sized marsupials being relatively abundant.

The coastal areas of West New Guinea tend to have relatively low population densities (except in a few areas in pre-contact times, and today around cities) and a rich natural environment with plenty of resources to sustain life. This includes all kinds of shellfish, wild fruit and vegetables, game and different kinds of fish. Until the recent introduction of some fish species, there was merely one in the highlands, with only endemic freshwater crayfish (*Cherax spp.*) as a natural resource from streams and lakes—especially in the Paniai area and the Baliem Valley. In spite of the rich natural resources of the coastal areas, the population densities are quite low. This might well be due to the prevalence of malaria, which kills many children and which was absent in most of the highlands, at least until recently.

Much of the transition area between the lowlands and the highlands remain thinly populated in relation to its area. In the north, the extensive Mamberamo Plain holds many different language groups but none of them are numerous. In the south, the central mountains reach down to Etna Bay. To the east, the mountains are further and further away with an ever-widening band of between 50 and 500 meters elevation, either devoid of people or thinly populated. In the past century, the Me have started to move into this zone until in some places they live closer and closer to the western coastal Kamoro. At West New Guinea's eastern end, the Muyu and Mandobo tribes fill this gap, with fairly high populations in the lowlands-to-highlands transition zone.

Trading: salt, cowries and stone blades

The area between the coasts and the highlands were crossed by a few defined trading patterns. While we have relatively good descriptions of highlands trade routes in Papua New Guinea, our available literature has but little information about coast-to-highlands trade in West New Guinea from the Pacific Ocean coast. (Trade in '*kein timur*'—woven cloth—in the Bird's Head is better covered.) On the other hand, we do have some information on trade routes and what was traded between the highland groups of West New Guinea.

This highlands-trading pattern was almost exclusively a network of east-west inland routes with salt, stone blades and pigs being the chief commodities traded. A few widely scattered locations in the highlands hold pools of salty water where absorbent vegetation such as banana tree trunks can be soaked. The soaked plants are dried and burned and the resulting ash shaped into standard-sized leaf-wrapped oval packages of some two kilos each. One of the reasons that the Lani (Western Dani) expanded to the west was the existence of salt springs in the Moni territory. There is no mention of any trade in salt between the coastal areas and the highlands, so these springs were the only source of this crucial product for all the highlanders. Unfortunately, this salt contains no iodine, as does sea salt, needed by our bodies. The lack of iodine results in a sickness called goiter, with an enlarged thyroid gland in the throat area and other worse symptoms. This condition can easily be cured by taking iodine in pills or by injection.

As with the salt pools, the few quarries, where the locations of the best stone blades were found, are also widely scattered. Most of the stone blades used for axes, adzes and for rituals in the central and western highlands of West New Guinea came from a place called Yalime, in the Wano linguistic area, just north of Lani territory. For the eastern portions of the highlands, the best quarry was found at Langda, In the Mek linguistic area.

While salt and stone blades were the most useful trade items, the currency of the highlands was mostly cowries and a few species of larger shells. The cowries varied greatly in their value, which increased according to their age and ownership history. The highest priced cowries could pay for a wife or cancel the human's life debt, that often resulted from warfare.

There are some ancient marine mollusks found in the highlands, as this area was ocean floor before being uplifted to form New Guinea's central mountain range. However, the money cowries all came from the coasts, mostly from Cenderawasih Bay. The shallow and turbid Arafura Sea in the south does not sustain this type of shell. So the cowries must have been traded to the mountains from west of Etna Bay or the Nabire area to the Paniai Lakes region and, perhaps, through many intermediaries. Some cowries could also have been brought to the Papuan highlands from the Torres Strait, either via the Marind-Muyu areas, or from the highlands of Papua New Guinea to the east of the current international border.

While the highlanders used bows from trees found locally, the best wood for making bows is the black palm. This tree is not found in the highlands and while some of the groups living at the edge of the mountainous areas traveled to the lowlands to obtain black palm wood, this was also traded with lowland dwellers. The main items offered by the highlanders for the cowries and black palm bows were tobacco and bird feathers.

In early literature about the highlands, there are many references to the antagonisms—sorcery, and fighting—between highland and lowland cultures, which probably prevented more extensive and friendly contacts. The Me group was in fear of attacks by cannibals from the south coast who raided just before dawn. These cannibals were probably the Asmat, although the two territories are far from one another. The closer Kamoro never had the reputation of being cannibals.

Distances, difficult terrain and mutual suspicions kept highlands-lowlands trade to a minimum in West New Guinea. There were no metal tools in the highlands prior to their introduction by Europeans beginning in the late 1930s and many areas remained in the Stone Age even for some time after that.

EARLY COASTAL TRADE WITH THE OUTSIDE WORLD

Kamoro canoes with sails, a very recent innovation on the south coast. The Malayo-Polynesian migrants to the north coast and offshore islands brought many innovations, including the outrigger and the sail. The south coast canoes are not designed for waves. They have not used outriggers and only very occasionally hoist sails.

Bundles of massoy bark strips tied together await export to Java from the shores of Lake Yamur. The bark of the **Cryptocarya massoy** *serves in folk medical preparations, perfumes and as a fixative for batik colors. Its taste is reminiscent of cinnamon.*

While the highlands of West New Guinea remained completely isolated from the outside world until the early 1900s (except for some trading contacts with the lowlands), the coastal areas had extensive dealings with cultures to the west for several hundred years prior to that time.

We have seen that the ancestors of the Papuans arrived from the west, over water. If they arrived over water, they could have returned over water: there are no physical factors such as ocean currents or winds that prevent east-to-west sea passage *starting* from New Guinea. Somehow we have to account for a crucial linguistic fact: a large area in Halmahera, Timor, Alor and a few other places speak a language more closely related to those spoken around West New Guinea than to the languages in the rest of Indonesia (the Malayo-Polynesian language family). It was probably through a long series of intermediaries, including Papuan language speakers to the west, that *'sirih pinang'* (the betel nut) was introduced to some parts of New Guinea from Southeast Asia as early as 5,800 years ago. But this introduction in no way attests to sustained long-range trade.

Lapita and Dongson long-range trading

While there was some local trade between offshore islands and mainland New Guinea, it was not until around 3,500 years ago that expansion and longer-range trade was begun by the Lapita culture. We have evidence for this from obsidian from New Britain (and Manus Island) found in Sabah, Borneo (Kalimantan) to the west and Fiji to the southeast. The typical reddish 'tooth-edged' pottery was distributed in the same range and perhaps even further to the east. This Papuan/Melanesian trade network was one of the earliest and most extensively known from ancient times.

Current archeological evidence places the origins of this Papuan/Melanesian (Lapita) culture in the New Britain/Manus islands to the north of Papua New Guinea. But there may have also been similar 'centers' on islands off West New Guinea, in places such as Biak and Yapen. However, as no excavations have been carried out in these islands, we will have to wait until expertise and funds are available to determine if West New Guinea's islands were also places of origin of this trade network.

After the decline of the Lapita trade networks around 2,500 years ago, we have concrete proof of exchanges between Southeast Asia, Indonesia and West New Guinea in the form of large bronze drums (and other bronze objects such as ritual axes). These were manufactured in what is now the northern part of Vietnam, between 2,400 and 2,100 years ago. Fragments of three of these drums have been found near Aimura Lake in the Bird's Head area, and other Dongson-related bronze objects as far east as Lake Sentani.

As further proof of this early trade and influence, we have bracelets of green, blue and brown glass, found in Balinese burial sites and dating from the early Metal Age. These are similar to the traditional valuables on Biak and further east, around the Lake Sentani area.

Metal appears almost instantaneously in Indonesia a bit over 2,000 years ago, but the presence of the metal did not extend further than northern and western New Guinea. While Papuans had no sources of iron ore, they did learn how to forge metal, but not until sometime before the year 1600. Using wood or bamboo bellows and imported iron, they fashioned excellent metal tools (mostly spear heads and machetes) and, later, silver jewelry from coins. Our first written source for forging comes from a Spanish account, written in 1606. It was at Triton Bay, on West New Guinea's southwest coast that these explorers saw iron forged into adzes and harpoons. It is highly probable that forging was introduced about a half-century earlier, from Tidore, via Gebe and the Raja Ampat islands.

It is most unlikely that the Vietnamese Dongson culture traded directly with West New Guinea, so we assume that the drums and other objects made their way to the Indonesian archipelago via a series of intermediaries in a west to east trading network.

There is no certainty of what was taken in exchange. We can speculate that the sought-after Papuan items could well have included bird-of-paradise feathers and, perhaps, slaves. These two items, along with several others, were to figure prominently in later trade from West New Guinea. The most likely reason for the trade from Asia to eastern Indonesian was the seeking of spices (cloves, essentially) and sandalwood.

Trade with Indonesia

Our next source of information for West New Guinea-Indonesian trade comes not from any physical evidence but from a poem-document called the

Negarakertagama, dating from the 1365. This text was written by Prapanca, a poet and court official of the Majapahit 'empire' of eastern Java that lists the 'dependencies' of this so-called empire. The easternmost area listed, Wunin (or Onin), refers probably to the southwestern side of the Bird's Head and/or to the Fakfak region and Bomberai Peninsula.

That Javanese traders visited southwest West New Guinea at this time (14th century) which was likely, but in no way brought under Majapahit control. Perhaps the principal product sought by the traders was massoy bark. Resembling cinnamon, this bark produces oil that has a sharp taste and pleasant smell. It also feels warm when applied to the skin. It was used in Java in traditional medicines for stomach and intestinal problems, and especially for pregnant women to prevent cramps and to help the healing process after giving birth. Other uses included cosmetics, perfumes and food flavoring for dishes like curries. Dyes used in Javanese batiks were also fixed (made more permanent) through the use of massoy.

If evidence of early (Lapita times) trade is lacking for Biak/Numfor, we know that these islands were the center of a Papuan long-range network of trade-and-raid. Bride prices on Biak required goods of foreign origin, which could only be acquired by trading or raiding. Raiding was more fun (and cheaper). And successful expeditions brought prestige to its participants. There are accounts of their raids for women, slaves and metal goods into the Moluccas, even reaching Sulawesi and islands of the Lesser Sundas of the Timor group.

Biak: Metal trade and forging

Metal tools were probably the most sought-after items by the Biak/Numfor raider-traders. The name of their culture hero, Gura-Besi ('besi' meaning iron) supports this fact. Gura-Besi traveled to the recently Islamized power-center of Tidore where he married the sultan's daughter. The descendants of this marriage became the rulers of the Raja Ampat Islands. Or so goes the story. Be that as it may, the Raja Ampat islands developed a stratified society, unlike most areas in West New Guinea. (Leadership was also primarily hereditary in the Yotefa Bay and Sentani Lake areas around present-day Jayapura.) In these types of societies, there are hereditary rules and nobles, commoners and slaves. Leadership, as in most of the rest of New Guinea, was very seldom hereditary and people were not destined to any class of society merely by the status of their parents. By and large, leadership in West New Guinea was won by individual effort, although as anywhere in the world, having a wealthy and powerful father helped out considerably. But one's own merits were more important. Not every child of a leader has the qualities necessary to inherit the father's high status.

Historical sources refer to Biak's loss of independence at the end of the 1400s, to the Sawai of Halmahera, who themselves were subjects of Tidore. But it is most unlikely that the Biak-Numfor islands were subjugated/conquered in the usual sense of these terms. The relation was more likely that of elder-brother to younger brother. The Biak/Numfor folks brought 'tribute' or gifts to the Sultan of Tidore and in return were given special clothing and titles. And it is most likely that metal tools were the most important items included in what these Papuans brought back home. Beads, ceramics and cloth were sought after as well, but were of secondary importance.

The Tidore connection was most helpful in obtaining metal tools for West New Guinea. Iron axes and machetes were brought to Ternate from the Banggai mini-archipelago off the west coast of Sulawesi. These were manufactured in four islands off the southwest tip of the same island, collectively called by the most appropriate name of Tukang Besi (iron worker). (There were other metal tools manufacturing centers on Sulawesi.) We must remember that there was never any 'making' of iron from ores in West New Guinea, only the forging of already existing metal.

Traders from Seram

Trade with Ternate was not the only source for imports into West New Guinea. Starting in the 1600s (or, perhaps earlier), several small islands called Seram Laut (located off the south-east tip of Seram Island) become trading centers, stimulated by knowledgeable refugees from Banda (after losing a war with the Dutch over control of the nutmeg trade) and Bugis from south Sulawesi. While trade in the Raja Ampat and north coast West New Guinea was mostly Ternate-influenced, the Seram Laut folks concentrated on the southwest coast. Starting in 1645, their long-range expeditions reached as far as the Trans-Fly region, in what is now Papua New Guinea, east of Merauke. While the Seram Laut traders occasionally traveled far, they concentrated on the area of the Bomberai Peninsula, south of Bintuni Bay. By inter-marrying with local Papuan women, they established Muslim trade centers in the region. (Swadling, 1996). This is the reason that today about half of the

Papuans in the Fakfak area are of the Islamic faith. Some Papuan villages in the Raja Ampat islands had accepted the Muslim faith in the 1500s, but these were few. The first recorded Muslim settlement there was in 1512 on Misool Island.

Trade items brought in at first by the Seram Laut merchants included metal tools, textiles, ceramics, gongs, brass and silver earrings and beads. Later, they imported elephant tusks and large Chinese porcelain dishes. In exchange, they took aromatic barks (especially massoy), damar (a gum used for lighting before the introduction of oil for this purpose), pearls, tortoiseshells, copra (dried coconut meat) and, most valuable of all, slaves. How these slaves were obtained was probably similar to the situation of Africa. While slave-seekers usually worked with local leaders who captured slaves from other groups; the merchants sometimes would also organize raids themselves. This led to obvious antagonism from the Papuan groups affected. Their hostility was sometimes directed to any outsiders, as European sailors found out to their dismay in the 17th Century and later. But the traders themselves also paid a price. In 1856, it was recorded that some 50 traders from the Seram Laut island of Gorong were killed on the southwest coast of West New Guinea.

A group of Amungme walk to the ceremonial ground in Aramsolki Village. They will participate in the 'tup' dance. The man in front is in traditional dress of penis sheath and wearing a cassowary feather headdress. He holds a bow and a bundle of arrows.

EUROPEAN ANNEXATION, NEW VALUES AND THEIR INLAND EXPANSION

7

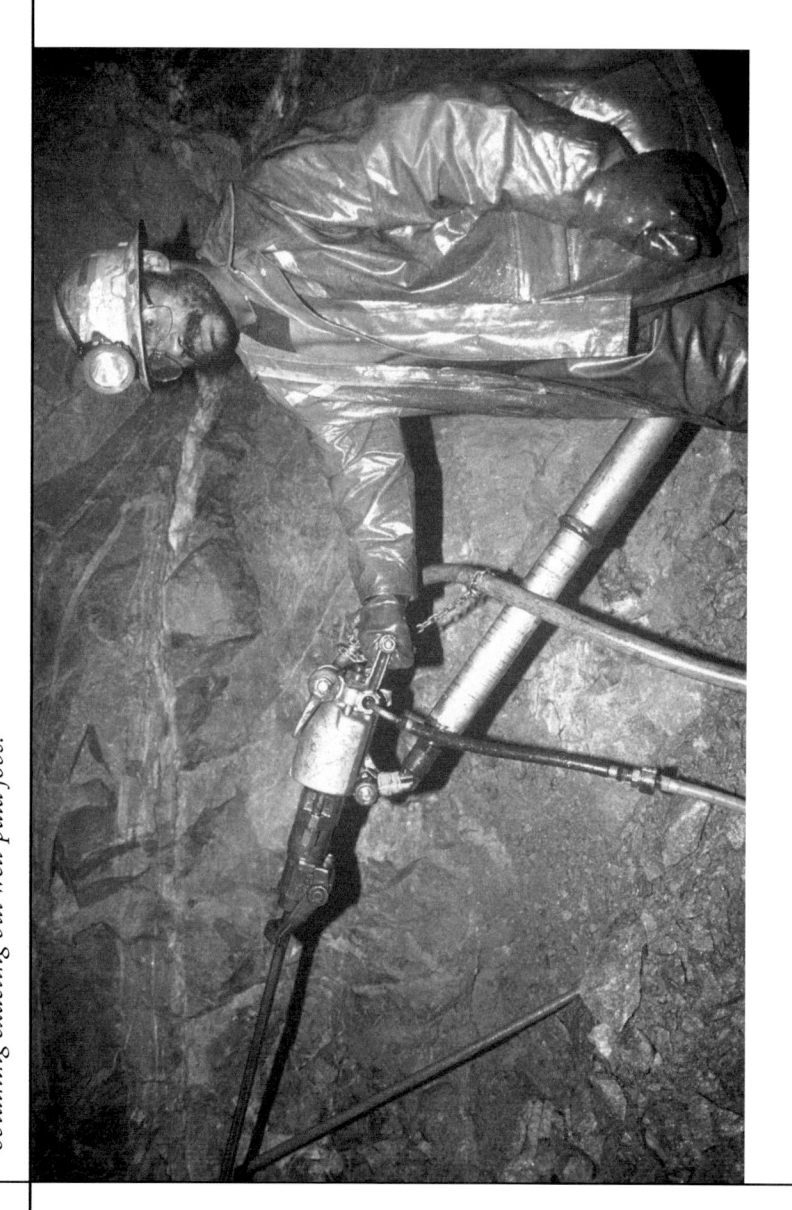

A Papuan miner works a power drill in an underground part of the Freeport mine, located in the central highlands mountains. With specialized training provided by the company, Papuans are obtaining exacting but well-paid jobs.

Colonialism introduced by the Europeans to West New Guinea had its good and bad points. Christianity displaced ancestral religion, a monetary economy has mostly replaced the traditional system of barter trade, writing complemented the spoken languages, and formal school education is supplanting the traditional one of learning by following the examples of adults and listening to their ancient stories. There were prohibitions carried out against warfare and cannibalism, sometimes successful only through the use of firearms. Indeed, superior weapons, along with Christianity, were key tools in the imposition of the new set of values. The introduction of the Indonesian language has helped to ease the communications between Papuans as well as outsiders. Europeans also introduced and enforced a legal system in which the concept of private or government land ownership, completely at odds with the traditional system of clan land tenure, that could only be changed through warfare. The concept of selling land in perpetuity was and, to a large extent, remains completely foreign to Papuan traditions and mentality.

The ancestors of the Papuans can 'speak' to their descendants though dreams and stories told from one generation to the next. These ancestors, over many thousands of years, have adapted to the different eco-systems found in West New Guinea, and today's youth can follow in their footsteps but only as long as they wish to remain in their traditional lands. However, when the modern world started intruding into the lives of the Papuans, the traditional lifestyle came under pressure to at least partially adapt to some new values that can be called 'modern', 'European', 'western' or 'Indonesian'.

Writing, did not exist in West New Guinea through most of its long history. Stories told by Papuan elders, once perhaps based on facts, became myths and legends through many generations of re-telling. Most Papuans' first contact with the written word was through the Bible, parts of which were translated by European missionaries and their Papuan helpers. On the other hand, the long history of West New Guinea has only been recently revealed though research (mostly by non-Papuans, unfortunately) and disseminated through writing. Research into the history of New Guinea is divided into several major disciplines, each of which require long years of study before these specialists venture into the field and attempt to apply what they learned: archaeology, linguistics, anthropology and genetics. And we have books and documents written by the early Europeans who first explored West New Guinea.

Unfortunately, we do not have any texts about what the Papuans in West New Guinea felt when contact was made, either with Europeans, or, earlier, with Indonesians. As most the contacts with Indonesians were not recorded, thus for evidence of the history of West New Guinea—at least for the past five hundred years—we have to rely on European texts. These are sometimes inaccurate or distorted, but often it is all we have, so they must be interpreted and not accepted as God's revealed truth.

The first explorers

The texts written by the first Europeans claimed to have 'discovered' New Guinea. Of course, the island was really discovered by the ancestors of today's Papuans and there had been trade and communications with Indonesia to the west and the islands of the Pacific to the south and east.

The early European voyages to this part of the world were aimed solely at finding the source of spices, especially cloves, which were extremely valuable in their far away homelands. The Portuguese were the first on the scene, having reached the clove-producing islands of Ternate and Tidore in 1512. Then in 1521, during Magellan's epic first circumnavigation of the earth, the chronicler of the voyage heard in Ternate that, to the east, there was a land ruled by the Raja West New Guinea, which was 'exceedingly rich in gold…' The information about the gold was false but this was the initial awareness by Europeans that a body of land existed to the east. The first European to set foot on New Guinea was a Portuguese named Jorge de Menenses who was driven east of his Ternate destination by adverse winds. He landed on the north coast of the Bird's Head, near Sorong, and called the island Ilhas dos Papuas, the Portuguese for The Island of the Papuans.

Competition for the control of the spice trade, initially between the Portuguese and the Spaniards, led to the next visit to West New Guinea by a European. He was named Alvaro de Saavedra and had sailed across the Pacific from Mexico (recently conquered by Spain) to help out a Spanish garrison under siege by the Portuguese at Tidore, and, not incidentally, to look for the rumored 'island of gold'. On his return from Tidore, Saavedra landed on Biak, which he called 'Isla de Oro', Spanish for The Island of Gold. Fortunately for the inhabitants of Biak, he found not the slightest trace of the precious metal. Another Spanish expedition looking for the island of gold was wrecked in Cenderawasih Bay and its seven survivors where captured and enslaved by the Papuans, thus becoming New Guinea's first white 'settlers'. They were later released after a hefty ransom payment was made to their Papuan masters.

The name of the island comes from yet another Spaniard, Ynigo Ortiz de Retes. He also sailed from Mexico, and landed in 1545. He named the island Nueva Guinea as he thought the Papuans resembled Africans of the Guinea coast. He found no gold and Spain lost interest in further explorations in the area. It took another half a century before another European sailed to New Guinea. It happened to be another Spaniard, named Luis Vaez de Torres. Heading west from the Solomon Islands, he sailed through the narrow gap separating southern New Guinea from Australia, thus establishing that these were two distinct landmasses. Torres made another discovery, as we saw earlier. Landing in a bay, which he called San Pedro de Arlanca (known today as Triton Bay), he saw and reported on Papuans forging iron.

The same year, 1606, the first Dutch ships sailed along the New Guinea coasts. By then, they were well on their way to take control of the spice trade from the Portuguese, Spaniards and the English. Captain William Jansz traveled along the west and south coasts of New Guinea, looking for gold and incidentally landed at various points, including the mouth of the Digul River. In 1616, two other Dutchmen, Jacob le Maire and Willem Schouten, surveyed the north coast, including the islands of Biak and Yapen. Then in 1623, Jan Carstensz, sailing in close to West New Guinea's southern shore on the Arafura Sea, sighted snow-capped peaks. His report was ridiculed once back in Europe as few could believe that snow could exist so close to the equator. The highest mountain he saw, now called Puncak Jaya, was initially named after him, Carstensz Peak, a name it held until recently. Nemangkawi Ninggok (the Peak of the White Arrow) is the proper name of this highest mountain between the Andes and the Himalayas at 4884 meters. This is the most acceptable name, as the Amungme have given it to the mountain, being the local Papuan group that owns the land rights there. Unfortunately, it generally goes by the new Indonesian name of Puncak Jaya.

After the sail-by in 1623, there was little in the way of exploration of New Guinea by Europeans, even along its coasts. Some famous navigators cruised by various parts of the island, but they seldom landed. The Dutch East Indies Company tried and failed to take over the small scale trading along the coast in massoy bark, birds-of-paradise and slaves. But this trade remained with Muslim merchants from the Moluccas until the early 20th century.

Attempts at colonization

Nor did Europeans have any more success in trying to establish a settlement. The British tried once, near present-day Manokwari, in 1793. Led by Capt. John Hayes, a small group built Fort Coronation to protect themselves against attacks by the Dutch or the Papuans. The aim of the settlement was to break Holland's monopoly on the spice trade. The Dutch did not bother to evict them but the Papuans, allied with malaria, drove the British out. The colony had lasted just one and half years. Later, the British were rumored to be planning to build a fort on Melville Island, off the northern coast of Australia, and not all that far from West New Guinea. That fort was never built.

But just the rumors were enough to get the Dutch moving. They had to have a fort of their very own on West New Guinea soil to prevent any other European colonial power from claiming a chunk of the western half of New Guinea. And if the Melville Island fort turned out to be just a rumor, another one heard was that the British were starting a trading colony somewhere on the southwest coast of West New Guinea, yet another false report. But the Dutch were decided by then. They were much better placed than the British as they had a government post at Ternate in the nearby Moluccas. The Dutch chose Triton Bay, near Kaimana, as the place for their settlement, centered on Fort Du Bus. In 1828, its initial garrison consisted of a lieutenant and 20 despondent Javanese soldiers (and their families), a military doctor who had no medicines against malaria, and a scowling group of 10 Javanese convict laborers who were there to do all the dirty work. The local Papuans were none too happy about this colony which was imposed in their midst without any preliminary agreement. (This lack of consultation with Papuans was to plague relations with outsiders up to the present.) So, as with the British fort, the Papuans called on their main ally, malaria, and eventually drove out the colony after it had existed—barely—for only eight years.

The first permanent European settlement began only in 1855, when two brave German Protestant missionaries, C. W. Ottow and Johann Gessler, built a house on Mansinam Island in Manokwari Bay. They had been sent to West New Guinea by a Dutch Protestant organization called The Christian Workman. They were the pioneers who established the bases for the their faith which spread very slowly along the coast of north West New Guinea and the islands of Cenderawasih Bay. It took another 50 years before the first Roman Catholic mission was established, at Merauke in 1905.

Ottow and Gessler learned the local language and with another missionary established four stations in the vicinity of present-day Manokwari, but they met with no Papuan enthusiasm to accept the teaching of Christ. During the first 25 years of the Protestant mission activities more Europeans died in West New Guinea than the number of newly baptized converts. The missionaries' deaths were not due to hostilities but to the 'rather prosaic martyrdoms of malaria' as one chronicler put it. However, the missionaries were not discouraged. Their unstinting efforts eventually led to the acceptance of Christianity along the shores of Cenderawasih Bay and the islands of Numfor, Biak and Yapen.

How The Netherlands acquired West New Guinea

In order to understand Dutch control over West New Guinea, we must take a brief look at some world history and European colonialism. Our glance will be brief and over-simplified, with many exceptions. Our purpose is to place West New Guinea in a worldwide, historical context.

After the fall of the Roman Empire, 1,600 years ago, Europe went into a period called the Dark Ages. Intellectual and scientific activities, along with most of the arts were restricted to small groups of monks and a few secular intellectuals. The nobility ruled over serfs, semi-slaves tied to the land they worked. Wars were the order of the day. While there were some notable exceptions to this bleak picture, it is generally true. No European country could equal the splendor of the Greeks or the Romans.

While China made very significant scientific advances, these were not much spread beyond the Middle Kingdom. It took the dynamic leadership of the Muslim faith to establish a wide sphere of learning, which took place in the centuries after the death of the Prophet Mohammed. Along with their conquest of what is called the Middle East, Arabs carried Islam. They converted and controlled the north shore of Africa and continued into Europe where most of Spain fell under their rule. Various centers such as Baghdad, Cairo, Damascus and Cordoba in Spain itself, all became centers of great learning: philosophy, mathematics, literature, astronomy and medicine. This Muslim culture carried on mankind's search for knowledge, continuing a tradition of inquiry, which had seen its best example in classical Greece during the centuries before the birth of Christ. The Muslims also controlled much of the world's long-distance commerce, which spread, along with their faith, to what is now Indonesia, among other places.

Europe began to 'wake up' from its relative intellectual slumbers during what is called the Renaissance, or re-birth. This was triggered when the Eastern Christian center of learning, Constantinople, fell to the Muslim Turks in

1453. Many of the artists and scholars from Constantinople fled to Europe, most of them to Italy. It was their intellectual stimulation, which woke up Europe from its Dark Ages.

Spain was re-conquered by Christians, with the final victory taking place in 1492, the year Christopher Columbus 'discovered' the Americas, thinking he had reached India or lands near China. By then, the Portuguese had sailed far south along the west coast of Africa, searching for an alternative to the land route to India, so as to by-pass the Muslim monopoly on trade to Asia. The Portuguese conquered Malacca, the main trade center in south-east Asia in 1511, and in the following year found the source of one of Europe's most sought-after and expensive imports: cloves from Ternate and Tidore and nutmeg from the Banda Islands. At the same time, Spain conquered Mexico and established its rule there, beginning the European colonial era.

How were the Europeans able to conquer distant lands, with few men when compared to the very able fighting forces of the local populations such as the Aztecs of Mexico? There were many factors, but superior military weapons and tactics were key ingredients. They also brought with them a powerful ally: smallpox, which wiped out great numbers of local populations. The Europeans, after many generations of exposure to smallpox had developed a degree of immunity, which the native people lacked as smallpox did not exist in the Americas then.

There were several motives behind the colonialist expansion. The search for gold, spices and other valuables were definitely the main reason. Also important, if more muted, was the 'search for souls', the drive to bring Christianity to the conquered peoples. This was in spite of serious theological discussions to determine if the Indians in Mexico had a soul or not. Those who backed the existence of the soul prevailed. Another reason for the European expansion was the search for knowledge: geographical as well as scientific.

Following the Portuguese and Spanish colonial drive, the Dutch focused their attention of obtaining the high-value spices from the chain of islands later known as Indonesia. By the force of firearms, organization and finances, they were able to establish a near-monopoly on the pepper trade centered in Sumatra and the cloves and nutmeg sources in the Moluccas.

The Dutch East Indies Company (often known as the VOC, or just the 'company') was unlike the Portuguese (whose motto was 'we seek spices and souls to save') and Spanish. The Dutch were not very interested in saving souls for Christ. They concentrated their efforts at enriching themselves. As long as they were able to maintain their monopoly on the spice trade, they cared for little else. For much of their colonial domination of Indonesia, they did not bother to conquer large areas. It was just too expensive and would cut into their profits. As long as the Dutch had their trade monopoly, locals could maintain their rule, religion and culture. It was only at times when Javanese rulers became too troublesome that the Dutch resorted to military action.

It was not until well into the 1850s that the Dutch decided to extend their effective control over most of what was to become Indonesia. And the last major area to 'benefit' from this expansion was West New Guinea. The main reason for the Dutch expansion was economic. As the anthropologist Dr. Ploeg points out, 'the imposition of [the expanding] colonial control had to do with the growing demand for a widening range of tropical produce and for minerals. That demand was first met by the so-called culture system [mostly in Java], and later by private entrepreneurs running plantations and mines.'

How West New Guinea became part of the Dutch East Indies

In 1660 the Dutch East Indies Company recognized the Sultan of Tidore's sovereignty over 'the Papuan Islands in general' and then signed a treaty with the sultan to keep all other Europeans out. The Dutch then tacitly acknowledged the sultan's right to send out '*hongi*' expeditions, brutal Tidorese-led tribute collecting flotillas of large war-canoes. These were more like raiding parties, robbing, raping and pillaging and not much appreciated by the Papuans who resisted when possible.

The 'legal' authority of the Sultan of Tidore over parts of West New Guinea were the bases for the Dutch claim to the western half of the island, as the sultan was bound by treaty to The Netherlands. But as West New Guinea was not a source of income for the Dutch, it was neglected. That is, until the British proclaimed a protectorate over southeastern New Guinea, at Port Moresby in 1884. In the same year, the German Imperial flag was raised on the New Guinea's northeast coast. The Dutch realized that they had to act if they were not to lose West New Guinea to some other European power. They had already claimed the western half of it to 141º East, a short distance from present day Jayapura and Merauke.

Bases for colonial claims

The idea of owning a land already inhabited by 'claiming' it with a few men through simply planting a flag and reading a proclamation was widely used by European powers to acquire colonies. These 'claims' were made possible only by the fact that 'might makes right' which unfortunately still exists today. Might means superior weapons, coupled with large-scale organization. Europeans had the weapons and the organization, which the Papuans lacked. Papuans were deficient of any large-scale, effectively led politico-military units. But even more important, bows and arrows, along with spears, do not carry any argument for long against firearms. Not then, not today.

Be that as it may, the Dutch-designated boundary at 141° East was agreed to by the British in 1895 and the Germans in 1910. Of course, the Papuans were not consulted. This international boundary line is still the same today, but now it lies between the independent (since 1975) nation of Papua New Guinea and the Indonesian province covered by West New Guinea. The boundary was drawn across language groups, which now find themselves separated from their brothers and cousins, living in separate countries. (The Europeans also drew arbitrary boundary line with no consultations with the locals in Africa, separating ethnic groups that should be in the same nation today.)

A crucial conference of the day's leading colonial powers took place in Germany in 1885. The Berlin Conference exerted pressure on Holland as the other powers had decided that claims to colonial possessions had to be secured by effective occupation. At the time, there was no Dutch occupation of West New Guinea, effective or not. Already in the previous year, in 1884, both the British and the Germans had begun to set up the administrative machinery necessary to control their colonies in the eastern part of New Guinea.

The Dutch finally established administrative posts in 1898, at Manokwari and Fakfak. Merauke followed in 1902, under pressure from the British. It seemed that the Dutch-administered Marind-anim were cutting off British-administered heads on the wrong side of the international border. The Merauke post was built to stop these Marind-anim raids. On the north coast, the small Dutch outpost named Hollandia (the future Jayapura) was not established until 1910. For much of the pre-World War II period, Dutch administrators on the ground were few and far in between. Aside from the few European 'controlleurs', mostly Indonesian 'posthoulers' ran a number of small outposts.

The Europeans venture inland

While the Papuans living in the interior of New Guinea knew their environment perfectly well, with specific names for most of the many plants and animals, this deep pool of knowledge was unavailable to the outside world. The lack of communications and language barriers kept the interior's secrets from all but its inhabitants. It took European explorers and scientists to reveal these treasures to the world at large.

Alfred Wallace, a most enterprising explorer, was the first of a line of distinguished scientists to visit West New Guinea. In 1858 he spent three months on the shores of Manokwari Bay, meeting the German missionaries and describing the plants and animals he found there. He also gives us a first hand glimpse of the Papuans, at the foot of the Arfak Mountains as well as on Waigeo Island. He wrote what is acclaimed as the best and most famous book about his work and travels, which lasted eight years—*The Malay Archipelago*. His best-known contribution to science was his finding an imaginary line separating Asian and Australian-type animals, later called the *Wallace Line* in his honor. This line, runs between Bali and Lombok in the south and between Sulawesi and Kalimantan to the north. He correctly suspected that the seas between these islands were too deep to have been low enough during the glacial periods for wildlife to spread: large land mammals like tigers and elephants could not cross from west to east and marsupials never made it the other way.

While Wallace never made it very far inland, that honor goes to two Italians, Luigi Maria d'Albertis and Odoardo Beccari. They spent many months in the Arfak Mountain in 1872, starting from Manokwari Bay. With Venetian beads for trading, they obtained many birds and insects whose existence was completely unknown to scientists. One of these two men, d'Albertis, needed all the strength of his strong character for his next venture. This was in 1876 when he led an expedition up the Fly River then under British administration, now in Papua New Guinea (PNG). Using a small riverboat called Neva, he reached an awesome 930 kilometers upriver. Among his problems were hostile Papuans whom he terrorized by launching fireworks over the river. His crew almost mutinied; he beat a Chinese assistant to death. But it took someone like him to put up with the difficulties of this type of expedition in those days. We have no idea of what the Papuans thought about Beccari (or any of the other explorers). Later on, many Papuans thought the first Europeans were returning ancestral spirits.

Towards the very end of the 1800s, when the Dutch finally established two administrative posts in West New Guinea (Manokwari and Fakfak), they began to realize that the German and the British in the eastern part of New Guinea had begun to explore the interior portion of their colonies. And the Dutch had done nothing. If other European powers were to be kept out of West New Guinea, Holland had to know what lay in the vast interior of their half of the island. The Dutch had to show the world that even if it was a small country it could rule the huge colony of the East Indies, now Indonesia.

Large-scale expeditions to the central mountains from the south

After some soul-searching about finances, the governor-general of the Dutch East Indies decided to send a series of military-led expeditions into the far interior of West New Guinea between 1907 and 1915. The leaders of these expeditions had strict orders to kill Papuans only in an emergency, upon being attacked. In the various reports on the results of these inland trips, some Papuans 'had' to be killed, but this was quickly justified and glossed over.

The first of a series of long inland explorations started off from the south east coast of West New Guinea. Here, a series of wide rivers allowed the large parties of well over 200 men to reach a fair ways inland before they had to start walking. The large numbers were required to bring food and other supplies to the forward teams. Thus the expeditions traveled up river systems that were named by them: the Digul first, then the next one to the north, the Mappi in its lower reaches, then its upper tributaries, the Wildeman (Dutch for 'wild man'), the Vriendschaps (friendship), and the Eilanden (islands). The towering inland mountain chain was the goal of these expeditions. While the Dutch had long known about snow-covered Nemangkawi Ninggok (Carstensz Peak, Puncak Jaya), they soon discovered another one, of slightly lower elevation. They named it Wilhelmina in honor of their queen and today it is called Trikora, rather than Pringgili, the name given by the local Papuans living nearby.

About the time that the Dutch were beginning to think seriously about inland explorations in West New Guinea, they received a most unusual request from the British Ornithologists' Union for permission to also conduct a large-scale exploration to the interior from the south coast. As Britain was a friendly country, Holland could not refuse this permission, but national pride was stung: the snow mountains had to be reached first by Dutchmen, not the British.

The first exploration trip inland took place in 1907, under the leadership of H. A. Lorentz. Accompanied by a strong military detachment as protection against potential Papuan hostility, the team started from the southeast coast. Then they were taken up the Noord River (North River, later renamed the Lorentz) as far as possible, and then continued on foot in the tropical rain forest. While the expedition reached a fair ways inland, they were forced to return due to illness, mostly beriberi, caused by a lack of vitamins. The team was also short of food and water. The expedition was considered a failure, as the team had not reached the Snow Mountains. But there were positive results as well. They made scientific collections of plants and animals, mapped a relatively wide area and established the fact that inland Papuans were different from those on the coast.

The second major exploration was also led by Lorentz and followed a similar route to the interior in 1909. Relations with a local group called Pesegem (probably Nduga or perhaps Dani) were quite friendly. The Papuans even killed two pigs to help feed the expedition during the early phase of the inland trek, and later traded food and artifacts with the Europeans. And most important of all, aside from collecting high altitude plants and animals (which they did not do on the first trip), the team made it to the snows (but not to the top) of Mt. Wilhelmina (Trikora). They had beaten the British to the equatorial snow, so Dutch nationalist pride was saved.

The next (and last) major Dutch expedition from the south, led by Franssen Herderschee profited from the experiences and geographical knowledge acquired by the first two teams under Dr. Lorentz. With the crucial help of Dayak porters from Kalimantan, the team leader reached the top of Wilhelmina in 1913. The jubilant Dayaks celebrated with a snowball fight. High spirits notwithstanding, the expedition's more ambitious plan to cross the central mountains to the Mamberamo basin had to be shelved as impractical due to limited supplies and time. This third major expedition was able to gather high altitude collections of plants (as the previous one did not collect above 2300 meters). They also recorded more and better ethnographic data from the Pesegem highlands Papuans.

During all three expeditions, the Dutch navy played a key role in bringing the exploring teams as far as possible up rivers while the military topographic service produced very accurate maps of this previously completely unknown region. Of course, 'unknown' only applies to the outside world. The Papuans 'knew' their region perfectly well but they had neither means nor any reason to communicate this knowledge to the outside world.

The British team

The poor British! Their 15-month long 1909 to 1911 expedition had an awful time of it, not reaching anywhere near their goal of Carstensz Peak. Their basic problem was that they chose the wrong river—or that the wrong river was chosen for them by the colonial authorities, bent on foiling any non-Dutch attempt to be the first to reach the eternal snows of the interior of West New Guinea. The British team was stuck with the Mimika River, which, as it turned out, did not reach anywhere near Carstensz Peak. Once they reached the upper limit of canoe travel on the Mimika River, the team found themselves separated from the high mountain range by impassable gorges. The expedition, with some 400 men, was just too much to keep supplied while the forward teams tried various paths to the north. During the very first week, a European member drowned. About 12% of the expedition died of disease or accidents and over three quarters had to be invalided out of West New Guinea. The personnel was a mixed one to say the least: soldiers from Ambon, convicts from Java and elsewhere, Gurkhas from Nepal, Dayaks from Kalimantan, occasional Kamoro canoe paddlers and reluctant porters, aside from the Europeans: seven men from Britain and a Dutch lieutenant. At the end of the 15-month ordeal, two British, a lone Dutchman, four Gurkhas and three escorts were the only ones remaining from the original 400. (Others, mostly Ambonese and Javanese, were brought in to replace most of the first group of 400.)

The failure to reach the snows was only slightly compensated by 2,200 bird skins of 235 species, many new to science along with six cases of mammal skins, endless tanks and bottles of reptile and insect specimens. The expedition made much of their one 'triumph': contact with an inland group in the foothills, of the Me or Moni ethnic group. They were (mistakenly) classified as 'pygmies' and much was made in Europe about their 'discovery'. Not much appreciated at the time, the expedition collected many Kamoro ethnographic objects that provide us with a first-contact description of this important coastal group. The British also accurately mapped a large chunk of territory of the lowlands and mountains.

In one way at least, the British team was more successful than the Dutch. Their findings were published in books and articles in the English language and were made widely available. The Dutch results were published in Dutch, a language understood by very few people then as today. No detailed accounts exist in English of any of the major Dutch expeditions. But even today, one can still purchase from the internet the two books published by the British team.

And there is a final chapter to the British effort: a year after the return of the 1909–1912 expedition, one of its main leaders, Wollaston, returned to West New Guinea for another try. Picking the 'correct' river this time, the Otakwa, he made his way inland first on this river, then by trekking north along the Tsinga Valley. He finally reached the central range: at the foot of the 'hanging' glacier, which ran down the south side of Nemangkawi Ninggok (Puncak Jaya). But not having the proper equipment, he failed to reach the mountaintop. That was left to a Dutch expedition, led by C. Colijn, which took place 23 years later.

Expeditions to the central mountains from the north

Before we look at the well-planned and executed trek of the Colijn team from the south, and its even more momentous consequences, let us take a brief look at what had happened on the other side, the north side, of the central mountain range. While the expeditions from the north had the wide Mamberamo area (the Lakes Plain) to cross, once they reached the mountains, the upward climb was considerably less steep than for the pioneer explorers attacking the mountains from the south.

Near the north shore of West New Guinea, the Foja Mountains constrict the great Mamberamo River into very dangerous rapids and these had to be mastered before continuing further inland. One of the early expeditions, led by the same army captain Franssen Herderschee who first climbed Mt. Wilhelmina (Trikora) was able to cross the Lakes Plain and enter the northern foothills of the central mountains, but could not continue further south as it was forced to turn back by illness.

After becoming familiar with the Mamberamo area, there were three expeditions of note that reached and penetrated West New Guinea's central highlands. Two expeditions run by the military and partially sponsored by the Netherlands Indies Committee for Scientific Research, had also been active in sponsoring the Dutch expeditions from the south. The first of these, led in 1920 by Van Overeem, reached the Lani (West Dani) living in the Swart (Toli) Valley but went no further. A year later, the second one, led by Kremer, also reached the highlands through the Swart Valley, but then went on through the North Baliem to reach Mt. Wilhelmina. Capt. Herderschee participated in this momentous trek, thus becoming the first person to have crossed West New Guinea along its north-south axis, albeit in two separate trips. During this expedition, the Swiss anthropologist Paul Wirz, spent two months in the Swart Valley and was able to gather a remarkable amount of still-valid ethnographic information, given his scant knowledge of the Lani language.

This expedition's route was close to the Baliem Valley, but no notice was taken of this most populated and largest of West New Guinea's mountain valley.

The team did discover a large lake, which was named for Lt. Habbema instead of its Dani designation of Yugi Nopa. This high mountain lake was to serve as the base for the 1938 American-led exploration, which discovered and trekked through the Grand Valley of the Baliem River.

The first use of an airplane in exploring West New Guinea

In 1926, an American-Dutch team, led by Matthew Stirling and the Dutch ethnologist, Le Roux, followed the Mamberamo upstream, then headed west along one of its two major tributaries, the Rouffaer. The team then followed another tributary river, the Nogolo, to reach into the highlands where they met a then-unknown group, the Moni, who lived just beyond the farthest settlements of the Lani or Western Dani. The two previous expeditions from the north were monsters of logistics, with 400 to 500 men in the field at any one time. The Stirling team solved this problem to an extent through the first use of a hydroplane called the Ern. This was the first time an airplane was used in West New Guinea. Ferrying supplies ahead of the main party was one of its jobs, which helped to cut down on time and the numbers of carriers needed. But even more importantly, the airplane could fly ahead to map out the easiest route, then ferry the advance team as far as possible, meaning where there was still enough flat water for a landing before the rapids began cascading down the steep mountainside.

This group did not have mountain climbing as a goal, but they did catch what they called 'spectacular views' of the highest peak, then called Carstensz Top. They established a camp in the highlands, and, unlike any previous explorers (except for Wirz), spent time with the Papuans there: two and a half months studying the 'pygmies'. They remarked that these mountain folks had a 'friendly disposition and calm behavior [that] contrasted strongly with the excitable Papuans of the Lakes Plain'. The expedition made a large collection of ethnographic materials which was equally divided between their sponsoring institutions: the Smithsonian in Washington DC, USA and the Netherlands Committee for Scientific Research. And more: a man named Dick Peck, the official photographer, shot 20,000 feet of motion picture film showing 'all aspects of the expedition and a good cross-section of native life'. By some miracle none of the film was spoiled by the heat and humidity.

The Colijn Expedition of 1936

By the mid-1930s, there was one major goal left for ambitious explorers of West New Guinea: the highest peak in the land: Nemangkawi Ninggok, Carstensz Peak or Top, briefly called Puncak Sukarno and finally, officially, Puncak Jaya. This task fell to three young Dutch mountain climbers, all working in oil exploration, and based in Babo, on the south shore of Bintuni Bay. The team was led by Anton Colijn; other members were Frits Wissel, airplane pilot and Jean-Jacques Dozy, geologist.

As with the Stirling expedition, this team made extensive use of an airplane. First and foremost, they made a route map using aerial photographs to find the easiest way to the base of Mt. Nemangkawi. Before the ascent was begun, a team from the oil company cut a track from the furthest place that could be reached by canoe on the Aikwa River to the base of the mountains. Unlike all previous expedition, this group wanted to stay small and move fast. Aside from the three Europeans, eight Dayak porters from Sarawak, all working for the oil company in Babo, were chosen as the only porters. It was planned to drop supplies from the airplane at two strategic locations.

The party made its way inland along the pre-cut route, then headed up and along a ridge, which led them to the Amungme hamlet of Opitawak. From there, the team descended to their base camp, the current location of Banti village. It had taken them just ten days to reach this point. Here, the airplane piloted by Wissel, dropped them a load of supplies. Another load was dropped in the Carstenszweide, a flat meadow just below the base of Nemangkawi Ninggok. This place is the current location of Freeport's huge Grasberg mine.

After dropping the supplies, Wissel landed his airplane at the mouth of the Aikwa River and hurried to meet his friends who had started their ascent from base camp up the Aghawagong River. He joined them just before they reached the Carstenszweide, where they set up their Alpine Camp. From there, the team climbed a short ways to the glaciers and ascended what was then the highest peak: the Ngga Pulu. Currently, this peak measures 4862 meters, but back in 1936 it was covered with some 45 meters of snow and ice and was thus then higher than Nemangkawi Ninggok, which measures 4884 meters. This peak, currently the highest, was not climbed until 1962 by a team led by Heinrich Harrer. This feat was made possible by the preliminary work of the New Zealander, Philip Temple, who did all the ground surveys and established routes but ran out of money before he could make the final assault. He joined the Harrer-led team and led it to the summit but the credit of being the 'first' goes to Harrer, the team leader. Such is life.

When the Colijn team reached the Carstenszweide, they immediately saw the most unusual feature of the landscape: a black outcrop of sparkling rock. Called Jelsegel Ongopsegel by the Amungme landowners, this high-grade copper and gold ore body was named Ertsberg (Ore Mountain, Gunung Biji) by the geologist Dozy and became the reason Freeport began mining in West New Guinea.

The Archbold expedition discovers the Baliem Valley

But if the Colijn expedition was the beginning of a great change for West New Guinea, there was an even more momentous one which took place two years later. An American millionaire with the most appropriate name of Archbold led this one. This man could afford any toy he wanted and he had a very expensive (and useful) one when he led his exploration of West New Guinea. This toy, called the Guba, was a hydroplane, and not a little one. The airplane had begun its career as a standard US long-range patrol bomber, and then was brought by a man far richer than our Archbold, the billionaire Howard Hughes. Mr. Hughes loved airplanes and had the interior of the Guba converted to a luxurious apartment so he could take his friends (and girl friends) fishing in style. Our man Archbold was of a different breed. He bought the Guba for exploration, not for showing off. Powered by two 1,000 horsepower engines, the airplane could lift three tons at sea level, an extraordinary amount even today. And best of all, the plane could land on land or water.

After two major exploratory trips on the eastern side of the island, Archbold was ready to take a close look at the highlands of West New Guinea. Other explorers had barely nibbled at the fringes of the highlands or, once, passed through quickly. There remained huge blanks on the maps—the highland areas of West New Guinea. While doing some preliminary flights to see where would be a good area to explore, Archbold was astounded to see the Baliem Valley. No outsider had ever seen this valley, the most densely populated on the island, holding at the time some 50,000 Dani. It was not only the dense population that was (and still is) impressive, but also the wonderful and most efficient ways in which the Dani farmer-warriors cultivated the land, with neat, regular, irrigated mounds growing bumper crops of sweet potatoes. An author on West New Guinea said that the Baliem Valley was 'the only place in the world where man has improved on nature'. Indeed, modern agricultural methods have not been able to improve the yields of the Dani farmers in the Baliem Valley.

The Archbold expedition was efficiently planned and organized. The team had the full backing of the Dutch civil and military administration. Funds were no problem, thanks to Archbold's personal wealth. It was decided to set up two camps. One was above the Baliem Valley near Mt. Wilhelmina/Trikora, on the shore of Lake Habbema (Yugi Nopa), at 3225 meters. The Guba, landing on the lake, supplied this camp. The other base was in the lowlands, in the Mamberamo basin, at 50 meters above sea level. It was located on the Idenburg/Taritatu River.

The straight-line distance between the two camps was about 100 kilometers. And the Baliem Valley was about halfway, elevation-wise, at about 1600 meters. Military detachments set out from both high and low camps to cut paths meeting in the Baliem Valley. Their presence, with firearms, would insure the safety of the civilian explorers who were to follow them. The team from the Idenburg started towards the mountains and shortly after they left the lowlands they had a pleasant surprise: a heavily populated valley and best of all, a lake which they immediately named Lake Archbold. (No one seems to have bothered to ask the Papuan name for this lake.) The best news was that the lake was large enough with a length of 1000 meters for the Guba to land, thus bringing them needed supplies. It was located at an elevation of 700 meters above sea level.

The two military parties eventually met in the Baliem Valley, followed by the civilian explorers from the expedition's high and low base camps. Once they settled in the valley, their Dani hosts threw a huge feast for them, killing many pigs. And here we get a glimpse of a Dani custom: the Dani elders and the expedition leaders ate the animals' livers in what might have been a bonding ritual. Mutually incomprehensible speeches were made. And pigs' blood was sprinkled on the foreigners. The Swiss anthropologist Wirz who participated in the Kremer expedition in 1921 in the Swart/Toli Valley also experienced this sprinkling of pig's blood on foreigners. According to the long-term American missionary of the area, Douglas Hayward, this ritual was performed as the Dani thought that the foreigners were ghosts. Perhaps they were the spirits of the Danis' ancestors? In the highlands of Papua New Guinea, the first explorers were taken to be the returning spirits of ancestors. Was this true in West New Guinea as well? We need the Papuan perspective on the early explorations by outsiders of their lands in order to have a more complete history.

But before we leave the 14-month long Archbold expedition, we have to add that it produced an important body of scientific work: botanical, zoological, and topographical, along with bits of anthropology. The expedition's 'discovery' of the Baliem Valley was also published in a very popular American magazine, the *National Geographic*. This widely read article was to lead to a glider rescue operation there during World War II. But more importantly, it led to American missionary interest in the Baliem Valley. They dubbed it 'the promised land'.

The Papuan view

What did the Papuans think of the foreigners who came as explorers? We have very little information on this, although there is much of it locked in the minds of elder Papuans who either still remembered these first contacts or have heard stories from their parents or grandparents. Just who were these strange beings, with white skins, clothing and much desired goods such as metal axes and machetes, plus a seemingly endless supply of valuable cowry shells? While the foreigners had a fair idea as to what they could find, Papuans isolated in their traditional lifestyle, had no frame of reference in which to place the foreigners who suddenly appeared. Were they human at all? Were they spirits and if so, good or bad ones? Or were they perhaps ancestral spirits? There was probably no agreement on this, as sometimes the outsiders were received with hostility, sometimes with hospitality.

The American missionary-linguist, Myron Bromley, recorded a fascinating by-product of the Archbold expedition. In the valley, an upcoming young warrior-chief named Ukumhearik met the team. This man 'sponsored' the outsiders' visit as dictated by local rules of hospitality, required to be 'given' to outsiders. This guaranteed no attacks in the area under his control. The Archbold team gave Ukumhearik some shells and when they left, these shells were 'consecrated as a major clan fetish'. Bromley adds that with these powerful sacred objects, Ukumhearik won a most decisive victory over a major enemy group after his own people had been nearly driven out of the area. Thus Ukumhearik became one of the few major leaders in the Baliem Valley.

We can offer another example, which may or may not have relevance for other groups. The Amungme received the visit of two first-time explorers:

the Wollaston expedition in 1913 and the Colijn one in 1936. This Papuan group has long held a belief in a better life on earth, which they call '*ha-i*'. According to this belief, there would be a time when their ancestors would return from the dead and inaugurate the good life, a sort of paradise-on-earth. There would be no more work, plenty of pigs for feasting, no more cold, no more sickness, no wars or any strife.

It seems likely that when Wollaston showed up in the Tsinga Valley, the Amungme believed that the party represented the beginnings of '*ha-i*'. Initially at least, the expedition was generous with giving out food and gifts. When they were ready to leave, a large group of Amungme preceded them to the lowlands. They brought very little food with them, probably in the expectation that the 'spirits' would provide for them. But there was not enough food for them at the expedition's base camp. Most of them died. Wollaston, a medical doctor, could not determine the cause of their deaths. Perhaps it was starvation, perhaps malaria.

When the Colijn expedition was ready to leave the Waa Valley in 1936, many Amungme wanted to follow them. This time too, some died of malaria but several of men survived and were taken to the Dutch base camp at Babo. Did these men go in the expectation of finding '*ha-i*' or just to experience the outside world?

Here I must add a very relevant comment by Dr. Chris Ballard of the Australian National University. In his review of the above text, he wrote to me saying 'Remember that the Colijn and Archbold expeditions weren't really very momentous in the overall scheme of things—yes, in terms of European knowledge on New Guinea, but not necessarily for Papuans—the 1918–1919 flu pandemic was probably of more consequence…". This comment points to the urgent necessity for Papuans to write their own history before it is erased from the collective memory.

The town of Enarotali lies on the shore of Lake Paniai, the largest of three lakes at the eastern end of the southern highlands. The altitude here, some 1700m. is slightly higher than the floor of the Baliem Valley. The first Dutch inland government post was established at Enarotali in 1938.

OPENING OF THE HIGHLANDS

8

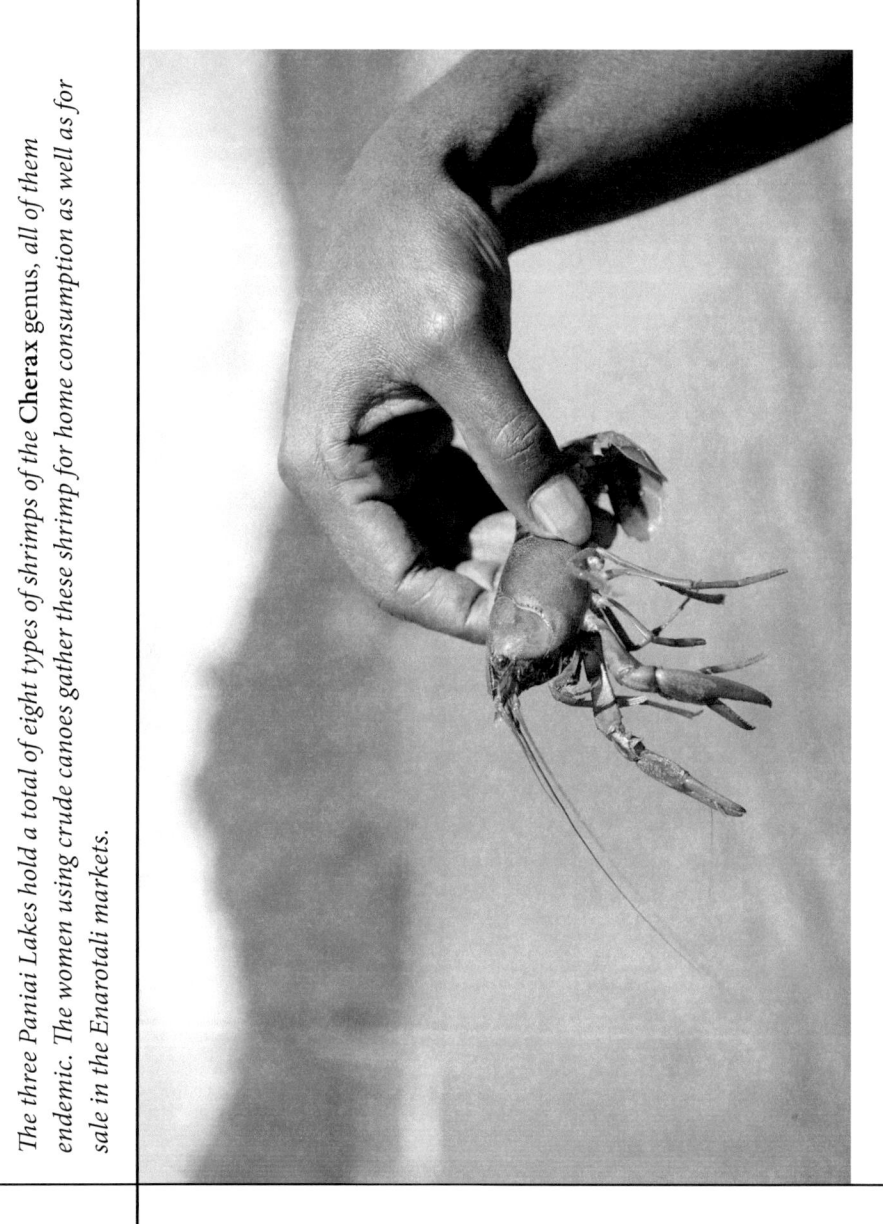

*The three Paniai Lakes hold a total of eight types of shrimps of the **Cherax** genus, all of them endemic. The women using crude canoes gather these shrimp for home consumption as well as for sale in the Enarotali markets.*

While we have seen many expeditions make their way to the interior of West New Guinea, these were all relatively fast in-and-out treks, which were not followed up by sustained contact. While geographical knowledge accumulated, with bits and pieces about the mountain Papuans included in reports, no expedition spent enough time due to a lack of a permanent base. Large numbers of the European expedition members had to be fed with familiar food, with many porters (who also had to be fed) straining finances and personnel.

Thus, in a very real sense, the 'opening' of the highlands started only with the establishment of the first government post, followed by missionaries, on the shore of Lake Paniai in 1938.

The 'discovery' of the Paniai lakes happened on the last day of 1936, during a flight by the pilot Wissel who we met during the Colijn expedition. The big metallic bird flying overhead caused panic both on land and on the lake where the ladies who were gathering shrimp jumped out of their canoes in panic. The event was deeply etched into the minds of all who witnessed it. In the pilot's honor, the lakes were given his name: the Wissel Lakes which was retained for many years, then changed when Indonesia took control. There are three lakes: Paniai, the largest highland lake by far, followed by the smaller but still considerable lakes called Tigi and Tage. This area is the center of the Me culture, a very large group of mountain Papuans, second in numbers only to the Dani and the Lani.

The Me group had been known by the coastal Kamoro name of Kapauku, for at least a dozen years before the Wissel fly-over. Father Tillemans, the Roman Catholic missionary, stationed with the Kamoro of Kokonau, had been in occasional contact with them. Unfortunately, we have no written records of Father Tillemans' meetings with the Me living relatively near to the coast. But a Dutch anthropologist, named H. J. T. Bijlmer has left us a good account of the initial contacts between Europeans and the far inland Me group. Tillemans participated in at least two previous major expeditions to the highlands.

The Bijlmer expedition

Dr. Bijlmer's interest in the mountain Papuans living inland from the Kamoro began when he joined a military patrol that made its way to the interior in 1931. This short trip traveled up the Mimika River, following the path of the British Ornithological Union 20 years previously. Contacts between the upriver Kamoro and the so-called Tapiro (probable Me, but perhaps Moni) continued, albeit only occasionally, with trade for tobacco from the Tapiro for metal tools from the Kamoro. The most important long-term result of this short trip was that it piqued Father Tilleman's interest in the 'pygmy question'. Father Tillemans found closer contact between the Kamoro and the Me to the west of the Mimika River, inland from the coastal village of Umar. From here on, the Kamoro name of Kapauku was applied to the Me ethno-linguistic group.

In 1935, Dr. Bijlmer and Father Tillemans set out from the Kamoro coast led by a mountain Papuan named Igogo. They were led up the Jera River, south of present-day Modio. Not far into the journey in the foothills, they already met Me tribesmen, who had built houses far better than those they had seen among the Tapiro. And, surprisingly, the men did not wear penis sheaths, but a small plaited covering of fibers tied to the genitals.

As the expedition reached the higher areas, Bijlmer writes that 'at 2,500 meters. the path continues through high woods, over fantastically eroded limestone, full of holes and caves. …we came to the top… a vast table-land (2,950 meters), covered with heather and tree ferns. …up to 3,150 meters. before descending in a northerly direction. The valley of Paniai… with the upper course of the Oeta (Uta) River before us, …is an important center of the Mountain Papuans'. (Bijlmer, 1922)

Dr. Bijlmer was wrong in writing that the Me people he met were the same as the Timorini (Lani or Western Dani) contacted by the 1921 Kremer expedition. He was also wrong in assuming that a ridge he saw in the north was 'an absolute bar to the mountain people' as to the north-west there was already a trade route to the coast to the vicinity of present-day Nabire. This was probably the trade route for much of the cowry shells used as currency in the highlands, at least in the western sector.

The expedition settled down to a place near present-day Modio, chosen for them by a most influential and hospitable local leader, named Auki. He sent for various groups of Me to come and meet the Europeans and it is likely that there was a delegation of the Moni with the Me. Dr. Bijlmer remarked that Auki's people did not practice the knuckle-click greeting, which had been mentioned by the British team when they met the Tapiro. There was a fair amount of information gathered during the visit with Auki, including their elaborate counting system. Dr. Bijlmer also began the decline of the designation of 'pygmies' for the highlanders, in stating that while stature was determined to an extent by heredity, it was also influenced by the diet. A Me leader, Weakebo who trekked to meet the Europeans, told them of a large lake located several days' walk to the northeast. This was Lake Paniai, waiting to be 'discovered' by the pilot Wissel. Auki's cooperation was much appreciated and remarked upon, but this was not benevolent: 'His commercial spirit left nothing to be desired!' This trait, common to the Me far more than other highland groups, was to be the theme of a book later written about them by Leopold Pospisil, an eminent anthropologist, and entitled *Primitive Capitalists*.

Enarotali: the first government post in the highlands

The news of Dr. Bijlmer's expedition and the discovery of the Wissel Lakes at the end of 1936, led to the beginnings of the Dutch government's first official presence in the highland. Dr. Cator, the assistant resident at Fakfak, cut a trail from the south coast, and then trekked over many weeks to reach Lake Paniai in December 1937. A short while later, a Navy seaplane landed on the lake. Another Dutch official, the police commissioner Jan van Eechoud also made his way to Lake Paniai where Father Tillemans joined him in June 1938. That same year Eechoud founded the first highlands government station at a well-populated area: the current location of Enarotali. In 1939 the legendary Dr. Jean Victor de Bruijn took over this post: indefatigable and highly intelligent, de Bruijn trekked far and wide, establishing government presence in the far western highlands. During the year after his arrival in the highlands, de Bruijn mounted an expedition to Kugapa, a Moni enclave in Me lands, and continued on to the heart of Moni country, reaching the village of Sanepa in the Kemandoga Valley. His contacts and the excellent relations with the mountain Papuans were to become essential to him during the upcoming war with Japan.

The same year the Dutch government post was opened at Enarotali, a Roman Catholic priest made his way to the westernmost extremity of the highlands. Shortly thereafter, the first American Protestant missionaries, of the Christian and Missionary Alliance (CAMA), arrived at Enarotali, after a harrowing 18-day trek through torrential rains from the south coast. Russell Diebler led this first missionary expedition (December 1938), and he was joined shortly thereafter by Walter Post. Their inland route followed the Uta River up to the limit of canoe travel, from where they trekked overland. Their wives, following the same route, joined them in April 1939 to help set up a school, learn the language of the Me and to make this mission post a family affair, as opposed to the lonely existence of the Roman Catholic priests. Father Tillemans returned to Enarotali in 1939 to plan the locations and establishment of Roman Catholic posts in the area. By 1941, there were nine Roman Catholic stations around Lake Paniai and Lake Tigi.

In June 1940, with World War II heating up in Europe, the Enarotali government post was closed and all Europeans were forced to leave. However, in November of the same year the government re-opened the Wissel Lakes post again and the missionary couple of Rev. and Mrs. Post were allowed to return in March 1941. Einar Michelson, another American missionary joined the Posts in December 1941. This was the same month that the Japanese attacked the US at Pearl Harbor in Hawaii, starting World War II in the Pacific.

Einar Mickelson: evangelical missionary

World War II was not to intrude in the Paniai area for another year and a half. This gave time for Mickelson to begin his work of evangelization in the highlands and, incidentally, leave us with some basic ethnographic data on the Moni group. Inspired by the Archbold article in the *National Geographic*, Mickelson wanted to work in the Baliem Valley, but that was too far away. But his church was eventually the first to open a mission station in that then-remote but highly populated valley.

Our man Mickelson trekked up from the Kamoro coast to Enarotali, suffering blistered feet most of the way (as did most others who made this trek). The Me porters who came to carry his gear from where the Kamoro left off, met him with the knuckle-click greeting typical of the highlands. In his baggage, Mickelson carried 50,000 cowry shells, the currency of the highlands where inflation was fast setting in: with the government and other missionaries also bringing in thousands of cowries, these rapidly depreciated in value. Eventually, a distinction was made between the 'new' and 'old' cowries which the Me could tell apart at a glance from their luster and coloration. In time, it took ten or more of the new cowries to command the same purchasing power as one old one.

After a short while, with the missionary Post family in charge of the base post at Enarotali, Mickelson set out for the Moni heartland, the Kemandora Valley. He had in his brief previous stay in the highlands researched their language and lifestyle, helped by Dr. de Bruijn who had made two previous exploratory trips to the Kemandora, in 1939 and 1941. Accompanied by two Indonesian men from the Makassar Bible School, Mickelson brought the Gospel to the Moni in April 1942. The location he chose as his base was a place named Wandai. This was near one of the most famous of the highlands salt springs and Mickelson had the opportunity there to meet some Dani who had come from the east to make salt bricks. He also met a party of Uhundunis (Amungme) who came through, found them friendly, and was invited to visit them—which he did, but not until after World War II. He explored quite far from his base at Wandai, trekking to the north of the Kemandora Valley and on further north to the Biandora Valley where he found Papuans of another language group, the Wolani. He did not spend much time there as a large-scale war was in progress.

During the year Mickelson spent in the Kemandora Valley, he made little progress spreading the Gospel among the Moni. But he was driven by his unshakable faith and convictions amidst the loneliness and isolation, the frustrations of daily life and the lack of interest in this religion by the indifferent Moni. Just when he felt that his ministering to the Moni was beginning to have results, orders came to evacuate. The Japanese had invaded West New Guinea, capturing all the coastal towns with the exception of Merauke. (Hitt, 1970)

The radio-relayed orders from the Japanese in Kaimana were clear: all Europeans in the highlands were to travel to the coast and surrender. The Japanese were waiting for them in Uta. The small white community ignored these orders. To make matters more tense, the Me were restless and a series of wars between them erupted. Dr. de Bruijn quelled these by fining the aggressors in shells and pigs, which were collected by his firearms-equipped police. It was then decided that a seaplane was to come and take out all the Europeans and their dependents, except for Dr. de Bruijn and four of his men. Time was running short. Some 60 Japanese soldiers had made their way to Mapia and were advancing towards Enarotali. Finally, a Catalina hydroplane landed on the lake on May 23, 1943 and 25 persons crowded inside, taking to the limit the plane's capacity for high-altitude take-off. Prayers undoubtedly helped, as the Catalina barely made it off the surface of the lake and then was able to gain enough altitude to clear the surrounding mountains. Prayers were also needed to escape the two Japanese fighters sent to shoot them down. They landed safely in Merauke, the only town in the whole of the Dutch Indies not to have been captured by the Japanese.

Religious competition: Roman Catholics and Protestants

We have seen that both of the major Christian faiths establishing their respective (basically similar but competing) denominations among the Me people before World War II intruded and all missionaries were forced to leave the area. There is no question that there was a degree of rivalry between them to win Papuan souls for Christ. This competition was not new in West New Guinea. However, with prodding by de Bruijn, the two faiths came to a 'gentleman's agreement' regarding the location of their respective posts: the Catholics agreed to remain only in the area that was around lakes Tigi and Tage (plus a small area near Lake Paniai) as well as the Moni enclave of Kugapa. The Protestants' main area of work was restricted to the vicinity of Lake Paniai but they were free to move to the east.

The competition between these two Christian faiths was not always so amicably resolved as in West New Guinea where it lasted well into the 1950s. Some of the worst distortions of Christianity had surfaced in Europe during the wars between the two religions, when people were murdered for belonging to the 'wrong' faith. Catholics killed Protestants and Protestants killed Catholics only because each side wanted to impose their version of basically the same faith. This was difficult to understand by anyone, let alone Papuans, even now. We want to take a look as to how this religious competition affected West New Guinea.

The Protestant faith, begun by Martin Luther as a reaction against some of the practices of the Roman Catholic Church, began in the early 1500s. The new denomination spread at least in part due to politics and power where religion became the excuse for wars between groups competing for control.

At the time of these wars, Holland was a colony of Spain, a staunchly Roman Catholic nation. The ensuing war between Holland and Spain was more for dominance than for religious reasons. The Dutch won that war and Protestantism became the state religion, although the remaining Catholics, who lived mostly in the southern part of the country, were more readily accepted (if still somewhat reluctantly) than in other Protestant-dominated countries. Many Protestants from France fled to Holland in order to practice their religion freely when Roman Catholics won their war with their fellow Protestant countrymen. In fact, Holland became known as the most tolerant of nations in Europe, insofar as there was more freedom of religion there than elsewhere. But as Dr. Ploeg pointed out to me, religious freedom in The Netherlands had its limits, as summarized by the pithy formula: 'freedom of conscience but not of worship'.

The Protestant faith remained the official one in Holland for two centuries, until the Napoleonic Wars in Europe, started in the late 1700s when Holland was conquered. France, and Napoleon practiced the Roman Catholic faith. At this time, Roman Catholicism was legally granted the same rights as Protestantism in Holland. These laws were also applied to the Dutch East Indies, in 1807. Unlike the Spanish and Portuguese colonists in Indonesia (and elsewhere) who put much emphasis on bringing the 'natives' into their Roman Catholic faith, the Dutch did not push their Protestantism. Only in Ambon and Manado did a fair number of local people adopt the their colonial masters' religion. The Dutch were more interested in profits than in converting Indonesians to the Protestant faith.

Two versions of Christianity in West New Guinea

In 1881, the pope decreed that the newly formed Missionaries of the Sacred Heart (usually abbreviated to its Latin initials of MSC) should start their work in Indonesia. Ten years later, there were Roman Catholic posts all over the archipelago, with the exception of West New Guinea. In 1881/2, the Jesuit order had opened two posts in the Kei Islands: at Tual (1881) and Langgur (1882). These became the centers for the spreading of the Roman Catholic faith to the south coast of West New Guinea. By this time, the Protestant faith had long been making inroads along the north coast and to influencing the islands in Cenderawasih Bay.

Father Le Cocq d'Armandville spearheaded the Roman Catholic drive to the south coast. In West New Guinea in 1894 he started a mission, near Fakfak. He baptized children, evangelized and explored the coast to the east. Father Le Coq's work met an untimely end when he died in 1896, either by drowning or being killed by the Kamoro. The Roman Catholic activities in West New Guinea then stopped until they opened a mission at the new government post at Merauke.

As the Dutch government extended control over parts of West New Guinea, more missionaries arrived, both Protestant and Catholic. In order to keep the conflicts between them to a minimum, in 1912 a boundary was established: Protestants to the north and Catholics to the south. This duplicated the split in the motherland, where the bulk of the Catholics are in the southern part of Holland and most of the Protestants in the north. This happy state of affairs lasted until 1927 when the governor-general in Batavia decreed that more than one mission could exist at the same location. But by then, it was difficult for either one of the competing faiths to make much headway inside the other's established territory.

European missionaries and mission workers such as lay brothers, and nuns were in short supply. Those available already had their hands full in the areas where they were already established. However, the Protestants were in a better position, as there were a number of Ambonese pastors available to take the place of European ones. No Papuan Roman Catholic priests were consecrated until after World War II. However, the Roman Catholic Church brought Kei teachers of their faith to staff schools in villages far from the posts where there were priests. And another Roman Catholic religious order, the Franciscans, began to send priests to West New Guinea in 1937.

The Roman Catholic faith spread in the 1930s to the Bintuni Bay area where an important oil exploration center was established at Babo. Many workers there were from the Kei Islands where Roman Catholicism was the dominant religion. The priests sent to minister to their flock there also worked on converting the local Papuans. Then in the late 1930s, a government program sent some 150 settlers of mixed Indonesian and European ancestry to Manokwari to establish an agricultural colony there, while a lesser number were settled in the vicinity of Hollandia (Jayapura). As a number of these new arrivals were Catholics, they established a foothold for their religion in the Protestant north coast of West New Guinea. A Roman Catholic post, opened in Arso in 1940, is still functioning today.

What concerns us revolves around the work of the two denominations in West New Guinea, especially in the emphasis of spiritual and material life of the faithful. In recent times there has been more convergence in the two versions of Christianity insofar as the material side of life is concerned. But before World War II there was more of a tendency of the Roman Catholics to tend to the spiritual as well as the material needs of their converts while the Protestants concentrated more on the spiritual side. But there were exceptions to this, especially in northern West New Guinea, where the Protestant church opened some schools and provided basic health services. (Hitt, 1970)

Thanks in part to government subsidies, the Roman Catholics established a more extensive school system in their areas of West New Guinea and promoted education in what was then called the Malay (Indonesian now) language. We do not mean to imply that the Protestants neglected non-religious education, but we are talking only about what was emphasized. The Roman Catholics also had better developed medical work. They also learned the local languages, with priests-linguists making important contributions to linguistic studies. Here again, please remember that we are writing about the period before World War II. Since then, the Protestants, through the Summer Linguistics Institute, have taken the lead in widely acknowledged and respected studies of Papuan languages.

WORLD WAR II IN WEST NEW GUINEA

9

A beach called 'Base G' received American troops that landed here in 1944 to defeat the Japanese who held the area of Hollandia, now Jayapura. The Japanese were not ready and were soundly defeated, with many casualties. General MacArthur made his headquarters nearby until he shifted back to the Philippines.

The Dutch government officer De Bruijn remained with a handful of soldiers (and lots of Papuan friends!) when the Japanese sent a detachment of soldiers to the highlands. Thanks to the loyalty of the Papuans, the tiny Dutch force was able to evade capture.

The Second World War changed much of the pre-existing political landscape of Indonesia. The Dutch could only offer token resistance to the overwhelmingly superior invading Japanese forces. All of the Dutch East Indies, including West New Guinea, was quickly overrun. The natural resources found there was one of the main reasons for the invasion: Japan lacked petroleum, rubber and many of the resources of the East Indies. These were needed for the development of the Japanese nation, to be taken by force. Japan wanted to become the dominant power in Asia, and for a few years it succeeded.

The Japanese advance into the Pacific was only stopped a short distance, less than 50 kilometers, from Port Moresby (the capital of Papua New Guinea), after some vicious, heroic fighting by Australian troops, greatly helped by local Papuans. Had the Japanese captured this city, Australia was but a short hop away. After the United States of America entered the war, the Japanese successes stopped short and a reversal began. General Douglas MacArthur led the allied troops in the reconquest of the Pacific, starting with the Solomon Islands and the north shore of New Guinea. But before we begin this series of victories, let us take a brief look at a much-neglected aspect of the war: the south coast of West New Guinea.

After capturing the town of Sorong at the extreme western tip of mainland West New Guinea, the Japanese forces advanced unopposed along the south coast. They reached as far as the Kamoro village of Timika Pantai, where a fighter landing strip was built. Two large shore batteries can still be seen at the nearby village of Kekwa. Patrols and temporary posts were pushed to the east, but no major bases were established beyond Timika Pantai. The allies retained control of Merauke, as the Japanese concentrated their efforts on the north coast. The Asmat area became a no-man's land between the two sides.

While the Papuans of the south coast may have been initially neutral or even friendly towards the Japanese, this soon changed as heavy demands were made on them for labor and to provide food for the troops. Some Papuans were tortured and even murdered because they did not comply fast enough with the demands or for not showing proper respect toward their new overlords. The Kamoro still remember kinfolk tied up on the shore to be slowly drowned by the incoming tide. Swift beheadings were merciful in comparison.

While there was no organized resistance on the south coast, a tiny but heroic anti-Japanese force operated in the highlands. We have seen that Dr. de Bruijn with four of his men stayed behind when all the other Europeans were evacuated from Lake Paniai. The Japanese soon arrived on the scene but by then Dr. de Bruijn was gone, melted into the scenery. That he survived and was able to report by radio on the Japanese troop movements and other activities was only due to the goodwill of the Papuans, Me and Moni, who held him in high esteem and helped out with food, porters and by spying on the Japanese. When the Japanese troops first arrived in the Paniai area, they bought a measure of goodwill with cowry shells which they distributed freely. But, they soon started behaving badly: shooting and eating pigs without payment, and killing some Papuans who they accused of collaborating with Dr. de Bruijn who kept eluding all their attempts at capture.

MacArthur and the War

With the departure of Dr. de Bruijn and his men, the war was over for the mountain Papuans. Just the opposite was true on the north coast. After General MacArthur had sufficiently built up his forces and supplies, he went on the attack. Victories at sea helped the allies in keeping their lines of communication open to Australia as well as the US. America's tremendous industrial might went into high gear to produce airplanes, warships, ammunition, and all kinds of arms and supplies, far outstripping the Japanese capabilities. As well as having control of the nearby seas, the allies soon established air superiority and eventually almost complete air dominance. As time passed, the Japanese became increasingly isolated in their outposts in New Guinea, with over-stretched supply lines and shipping mostly blown out of the water. The situation allowed MacArthur to take advantage of the mobility of his forces to concentrate firepower wherever he wanted. But there were some 55,000 hardened Japanese troops on the north shore of New Guinea, still backed by considerable air power and substantial naval forces based in the secure waters of the Moluccas.

The heavy fighting that began in the spring of 1944, put New Guinea on the map for much of the world. After neutralizing or bypassing Japanese troops on the northwest coastal side of the island, MacArthur was ready for a major move: establishing a large base, far inside enemy territory, from which to carry the fight forward. His choice fell on Hollandia (now Jayapura), a major Japanese military base. Thanks to intercepted communications and broken codes, MacArthur learned of the defensive weakness of the Hollandia garrison. While some 10,000 soldiers were stationed there, only about one fifth were combat soldiers.

The Battle of Hollandia began with 1,200 US Air Force airplanes wiping out the Japanese air fleet at Sentani, destroying over 300 of the Nippon planes. Only 25 still-usable aircraft were left. Then came the landing, at the time the largest operation in the Pacific. The allies amassed 217 ships and some 80,000 men, led by 50,000 combat troops. While the disembarkation was chaos in the rain, waves and difficult terrain, it had caught the Japanese unprepared and resistance was mercifully light. The beachheads, from Hollandia to Tanah Merah, were secured on April 22, 1944. MacArthur and his staff celebrated, not as Russians would have with vodka, or Australians with cold beers, but the American way: ice cream sodas. It was their due: military historians consider the Battle of Hollandia as a model of strategic maneuver. While only 152 lives were lost (and 1057 wounded) by the invading forces, some 3,300 Japanese were killed and 611 captured. The remaining 6,000 Japanese soldiers tried to escape 200 kilometers overland to Sarmi, one of their bases on the coast to the west. But disease and starvation claimed most of them, with only about 1,000 reaching relative safety at Sarmi.

The army corps of engineers reinforced the Japanese-built airstrips in Sentani so that they could handle the long-range B29 Superfortress bombers. Some 240 kilometers of airstrips and roads were laid, much still in use today. Sides of mountains were carved away, bridges and culverts built across rivers, gravel and stone poured into swamps to support highways. Overnight, Hollandia(Jayapura) mushroomed from a small, sleepy little town to a city of 250,000, more than one third of the entire population of West New Guinea at the time. It became one of the war's great military bases, with most of the southwest Pacific command operating there during the summer of 1944. The huge airfield complex at Lake Sentani became home to 1,000 airplanes of all sorts. An almost equal number of ships ferried countless tons of supplies and equipment. Humboldt Bay, with hundreds of ships linked to each other by catwalks and lit up at night, was described by war correspondents as 'a city at sea.'

There is very little about Papuans in the Hollandia records of the allied forces. But one event did bring them into focus, for the armed forces as well as the world at large. It might have received wide publicity, as it was a diversion from the brutal war which was still a long ways from being won. During their flights around West New Guinea, the air force pilots re-discovered the Baliem

Valley. The hidden valley's lush beauty and exotic setting promptly resulted in the name of 'Shangri-La', a sort of mythical paradise on earth. (The name came from a 1933 novel by James Hilton to describe a remote, beautiful, imaginary place.) Soon, military personnel on leave, men and women, were taken on aerial 'joy rides' to see the Baliem. But one of these flights crashed just outside the valley, killing everyone except two men and a female nurse. Their rescue was a major endeavor, requiring glider planes being towed off the ground. The oh-so-picturesque Dani warriors certainly attracted the attention of the rescuers, but there was no hostility between the Dani and the Americans, people worlds apart. Another *National Geographic* article spread the story with all the elements of "adventure-among-the-savages" (who were really not savage at all, except in western eyes).

Beyond Hollandia

Thanks to quick work by the Army Corps of Engineers and proper soils, the Sentani bomber base was quickly completed, enabling the Allied onslaught to move forward. It was not to be as easy as capturing Hollandia. Especially not in Biak.

As a first step, the Allies set their sights on the Japanese airfield in Wakde Island, which fell after four days of bitter fighting. The score was lopsided in favor of the Allies who lost only 40 of their men against 760 Japanese killed. More tough fighting was needed to secure the shores of Maffin Bay on the mainland opposite Wakde, essential as a forward staging area. Here again, superior and concentrated firepower took its toll: some 4,000 Japanese killed (but only 75 prisoners) at the cost of 415 US lives. While the particular unit in charge, the Tornado Task Force secured all-important positions, at the end of the war there were still some Japanese soldiers holed up near Sarmi.

Despite ever increasing Allied control of the air and sea lanes, the Japanese tried to send 20,000 troops as re-enforcement to West New Guinea from China. They never made it. Allied submarines sank four of the transport ships, drowning half of the Japanese. The rest of the troop carriers fled.

The next Allied objective was Biak Island, which stopped the US-led blitzkrieg cold.

The Japanese defense of Biak was, according to a US general, 'based on brilliant appreciation and use of the terrain.' Aerial photos taken from reconnaissance airplanes failed to detect the backbone of the defenses: the network of caves. Tunnels connected many of these caves. Stone formations inside the caves made them near impregnable as defensive positions. The battle of Biak soon became a nightmare for the Allies.

The Japanese allowed the Allied troops to land at Bosnik with little opposition. But this was a ploy devised by the Japanese commander, Colonel Naoyuki Kuzume. He held back his forces until the US troops had advanced to rugged terrain beyond the beaches. Then the Japanese struck back from the dominating cliff-cave hideouts that were located above the advancing Allied troops. They were free to choose their location and position and allowing for a quick retreat to shift the battle elsewhere. This was especially effective at night. Mountain guns and mortars were brought out of the caves but before morning these were hidden in the caves again. The savage Japanese counter-attack succeeded in driving a wedge between the beachhead and the invading forces. The situation was critical for the Allies until reinforcements arrived, but even then the going remained difficult. The soldiers suffered from the intense heat and a scarcity of water. All the tactics and weapons in the Allied arsenal were needed. Especially effective were the flame-throwers used after the cave-hideouts were located. Especially when a cocktail of aviation fuel and TNT explosives were poured into the caves as well.

The ultimate Allied objective was the three airfields at Mokmer (one of which would later become Frans Kaisiepo Airport), Boroke and Sorido. These were eventually captured and effective Japanese resistance ended by June 1944. The final toll was some 400 US soldiers killed, along with 7,400 Japanese, many of whom committed ritual suicide rather than surrender. Only 220 of them were captured alive.

The Papuans hunted down isolated individual Japanese soldiers and small groups who fled and hid in the jungle from Biak. There was no love lost between the inhabitants of the island and the Japanese who had tortured and killed many of them, especially while suppressing a messiah-cult earlier (the Koreri-cult movement).

The Allies quickly developed the airfields on Biak for their heavy bombers. From there, as well as from Wakde and Numfor, the Far Eastern Air Force was in a position to strike at the Japanese bases in much of Indonesia. But there was still a bit of work left. This was the last offensive in West New Guinea, on the northern shore of the Bird's Head. Amphibious landings at Sansapor and Mar were unopposed. These beachheads were only 150 kilometers west of Manokwari, the headquarters of the Japanese 2nd Army. Quick work by engineers soon resulted in operational airfields. Manokwari was neutralized in the sense that no supplies or reinforcements could be brought in as the Allies controlled the air and the seas. With no fighter or bombers left there and no warships or fuel, the Japanese at Manokwari waited out the war, no longer an effective fighting force.

As far as West New Guinea was concerned, in just four short months, from April to July 1944, the whole north coast had fallen to the Allies.

The Allies did not bother with any battles on the south coast. The airfield at Babo was bombed and no operational Japanese warplanes were left. With no aircraft and no supplies, the other Japanese forces such as those in Kaimana and Timika Pantai were forced to wait until the final Japanese surrender. There was no reason for the Allies to fight them. The US-led troops were set on their next major objective, Morotai Island off the north coast of Halmahera. From there, it was on to the Philippines and the final victory.

For Indonesia and West New Guinea, World War II resulted in major consequences. It showed that the Dutch forces could be defeated. This set the stage for the independence of Indonesia.

BIBLIOGRAPHY

Archbold, R., A.L. Randall and L.J. Brass. 1942. Results of the Archbold Expeditions. Summary of the 1938–1939 New Guinea Expedition. No. 41. *Bulletin of the American Museum of Natural History* 79(3): 197–288.

Ballard, Chris, Steven Vink and Anton Ploeg. 2001. *Race to the Snow.* Amsterdam: Royal Tropical Institute. Amsterdam.

Ballard, Chris. 2001a. A.F.R. Wollaston and the 'Utakwa River Mountain Papuans' skulls. *The Journal of Pacific History* 36 (1): 117–126

Ballard, C. at al, (eds.) 2005. The sweet potato in Oceania: A reappraisal. Ethnography Monographs 19/Oceania Monograph 56, University of Sydney. Sydney.

Barrau, J. 1959. The sago palm & other food plants of marsh dwellers in the South Pacific Islands. *Economic Botany* 13:151–62.

Bijlmer, H.J.T. 1922. (Reprint University of Michigan Library, 2015) *Anthropological results of the Dutch scientific central New-Guinea expedition Ac 1920*, followed by an essay on the anthropology of the Papuans. EJ Brill, Leiden.

Boelaars, J. H. M. C. 1981. Head-Hunters About Themselves. In *Verhandelingen van het Koninklijk Instituut voor Taal-, Land-, en Volkenkunde.* (92). Martinus Nijhoff, The Hague.

Bulmer, Ralph. 1968. The Strategies of Hunting in New Guinea. In *Oceania* 38:302–318.

Earl, George Windsor. 1853. *The Native Races of the Indian Archipelago—Papuans.* London: Hippolyte Bailliere.

Ellenberger, J. 1983. A century of '*hai*' movements among the Damal of Irian Jaya'. In W. Flannery (ed.), *Melanesia: a selection of religious movements case studies and reports*, p. 104–110. The Melanesian Institute, Goroka.

Flannery, T. 1995. *The Mammals of New Guinea*. Reed Books, Chatswood, Australia.

Haberle, S. G., G. S. Hope and Y. de Fretes. 1991. Environmental Change in the Baliem Valley, Montane Irian Jaya, Republic of Indonesia. *Journal of Biogeography* (1991) 18:25–40.

Herdt, Gilbert H. 1993. *Ritualized Homosexuality in Melanesia.* University of California Press, Berkeley.

Hitt, Russell. 1970. *Cannibal Valley.* Zondervan, Ann Arbor, Michigan.

Kamma, Freerk C. and Simon Kooijman. 1973. *Romawa Forja Child of Fire.* EJ Brill, Leiden.

Larsen, G. 1987. *The Structure and Demography of the Cycle of Warfare among the Ilaga Dani of Irian Jaya*, unpublished PhD dissertation, The University of Michigan.

May, R. J. and Hank Nelson (eds.). 1982. *Melanesia: Beyond Diversity.* Research School of Pacific Studies, Canberra, Australian National University.

Miklouho-Maclay, N. 1982. *Travels to New Guinea.* Progress Publishers, Moscow.

Mickelson, Einar H. 1969. *God Can.* No publishing information.

Moore, Clive. 2004. *Crossing Boundaries and History.* University of Hawai'i Press.

Muller, Kal. 1996. *Indonesian New Guinea.* Periplus Editions, Singapore.

Muller, Kal. 2006. *Keragaman Hayati Tanah Papua.* UNIPA, Manokwari.

Muller, K. and Y. Omabak. 2008. *Amungme. Tradition and Change in the highlands of Papua.* P.T. Freeport Indonesia, Indonesia.

Paijmans, K. (ed.) 1976. *New Guinea Vegetation.* Australian National University Press, Canberra.

Pawley, A. (et al, eds.) 2005. *Papuan Pasts.* Australian National University, Canberra.

Petrequin, P. and Anne-Marie Petrequin. 2000. *Ecologie d'un outil: l'hache de pierre en Irian Jaya (Indonesie).* CNRS Editions, Paris.

Podolefsky, A. 1984. Contemporary warfare in the NG Highlands. *Ethnology* 23(2): 73–87.

Pospisil, L. 1978. *The Kapauku Papuans of West New Guinea.* Holt, Rinehart and Winston, New York.

Ruddle, Kenneth (et al. eds.) 1978. *Palm Sago. A Tropical Starch from Marginal Lands.* University of Hawaii, East-West Center.

Sillitoe, Paul. 1998. *An Introduction to the Anthropology of Melanesia.* Cambridge University Press.

Silzer, P. 1991. *Index of Irian Jaya Languages.* Summer Institute of Linguistics, Jayapura

Souter, G. 1967 New Guinea. *The Last Unknown.* Angus Robertson, Sydney.

Spriggs, Matthew 1997. *The Island Melanesians.* Blackwell.

Swadling, Pamela. 1996. *Plumes from Paradise.* Papua New Guinea National Museum.

Szalay, A. 1999. *Maokop. The montane cultures of central Irian Jaya: environment, society, and history in highland New Guinea.* Unpublished PhD dissertation, University of Sydney.

Taafe, Stephen R. 1998. *MacArthur's Jungle War.* University Press of Kansas.

Taylor, Paul Michael 2006 . "Introduction: Revisiting the Dutch and American New Guinea Expedition of 1926." Essay 1 In *By Aeroplane to Pygmyland: Revisiting the 1926 Dutch and American Expedition to New Guinea*, by Paul Michael Taylor. http://www.sil.si.edu/expeditions/1926/essays, Smithsonian Institution Libraries, Digital Editions, 2006, Washington D.C.

Wallace, A.R. (1869) 1983. *The Malay Archipelago.* Graham Brash. Singapore.

Watson, J. B. (ed.) 1964. New Guinea. The Central Highlands. Special publication of the *American Anthropologist* 66(4).

Wollaston, A.F.R. 1912. *Pygmies and Papuans.* John Murray. London.

Zuckoff, M. 2011. *Lost in Shangri-La. A True Story of Survival and Adventure and the Most Incredible Rescue Mission of World War II.* Harper Collins, New York.